Stories, Advice, and Humor for Living Anywhere

CHOOSE to MOVE

Ann Cabot

NEW ARTS PUBLISHING
AUSTIN, TEXAS

CHOOSE to MOVE

By Ann Cabot

All rights reserved. No part of this book may be reproduced or utilized in any form or by any means, electronic, or mechanical, including photocopying, or recording, or by an information storage and retrieval system, without permission in writing from the author.

Copyright © Ann Cabot, 2005 Choose to Move. First Edition.

New Arts Publishing, Austin, Texas
www.newartspublishing.com

ISBN: 0-9770046-4-3

Senior Editor: Barbara Foley

Editing: Barbara Foley, Brad Fregger

Manuscript Preparation: Jennifer Smith

Interior Layout: Louanne Jones

Cover and interior design © TLC Graphics, www.TLCGraphics.com
Design by Monica Thomas

Cataloging-in Publication Data

Cabot, Ann, 1944-
  Choose to move : stories, advice and humor for living anywhere
p. cm.

  I. Relocation-United States II. Moving-Household—Memoir
III. Travel-United States IV. Moving-Personal Actions
V. Residential mobility-United States

ISBN: 0-9770046-4-3

HF 5549.5 C47   2005928325
648.9 C813

Dedication

Many people contributed to my incredible journey. To them I humbly and gratefully dedicate this book.

To my precious son Eric, who just won't quit moving me to higher heights.

To my brother Paul, who supports my every turn in the road.

To my family of supporters who trekked this whole story tear by tear and triumph by triumph.

To my parents who would have been proud and amazed at this accomplishment but would have discouraged me at every juncture. They played a huge, positive role in my being up to life's challenges.

To all the friends I made along my journey.

To every boss that gave me a job and saw me leave sooner than they wanted.

To every landlord who trusted me to rent their living space.

To all the mechanics who kept my car roadworthy so I could drive in strange towns.

To all the seamstresses who hemmed and mended my wardrobe to perfectly fit my imperfect body.

To all the dentists and doctors who gave me their best care as I passed through their territories.

CHOOSE TO MOVE

To all the *first friends* who met me on Day One with open arms.

To every post office worker who changed my address and held, forwarded, shipped, delivered, and processed letters and care packages to and from friends.

Thank you, one and all!

I also dedicate this book to every brave-hearted soul who entertains the idea of changing places and to every extra-brave-hearted soul who actually does it. You won't be sorry!

Acknowledgements

I wish to acknowledge the people who have helped transform my writings into a real book. Tami Dever was the first person in my life who knew how to publish a book and was willing to mentor me in that process. Without her help, I would never have started down the road to publishing. Barbara Foley was the patient and thoughtful editor who made the book readable. And without the tireless and enthusiastic encouragement and technical advice of Mindy Reed, I might have given up midway. Her meticulous proofing was a tremendous help. Monica Thomas and Louanne Jones gave their time and professional best for this effort. I wish to thank each and every one of you for your contributions to the success of this book. And to my mentor and life-long friend, Pamela Brown, who weekly kept my eye on the prize of a finished book, I say a heartfelt thank you.

Table of Contents

Introduction ix

How I Began Moving ❖ How This Book Is Organized ❖
Unique Perspectives of This Book ❖ How This Book Came to Be

Part One: Getting Ready

Chapter 1   Deciding to Go and Deciding Where 3

Deciding to Go ❖ Knowing Your Reasons and Resources ❖
Deciding Where to Go ❖ The World Is as We Are ❖
My First Move: Orlando, Florida, to Austin, Texas

Chapter 2   Leaving 23

Personal Belongings: Keepers or Leavers ❖
House: Rent, Sell, or Maintain? ❖ Vehicle: Keep or Sell ❖
Leaving Friends ❖ Leaving Family ❖
Leaving Professional and Personal Services ❖
Leaving Familiar Things ❖ Leaving My Home and Belongings ❖
Leaving My Friends ❖ Leaving My Family

Part Two: Creating the Right Living Conditions

Chapter 3   Housing in Your New Community 59

Choosing a New Home ❖ Weather ❖ Specifics of Home Selection

Chapter 4   New Town, New Job 83

Ideas to Ponder When Job Hunting ❖ Employment Opportunities ❖
Making a Career Change ❖ Do I Find a Job Before or After I Arrive? ❖
Being Without a Job

vii

Chapter 5   Making Friends 103

Suggestions for Finding Friends ❖ Types of Friends ❖ Solitude Solutions

Chapter 6   Getting Through the Low Feelings 125

What Affects Mood During a Move ❖ Changing Your Mood ❖
Remembering the Purpose for Moving ❖ Going Back for a Visit ❖
Health ❖ Keeping It Light

Part Three: Seeing How Far You've Come

Chapter 7   Expanding Your Territory 151

New Territory to Explore ❖ New Interests and Activities to Try ❖
New People to Meet ❖ New Foods to Enjoy

Chapter 8   The Incredible Rewards of Moving 169

Unique Rewards ❖ Twelve Major Rewards

Chapter 9   Thriving Anywhere 185

Staying Where You Are ❖ Moving Back to Your Hometown ❖
Moving to a New Place ❖ Other Influencing Factors ❖
The World Is as We Are ❖ In the Beginning

Epilogue 203

Bibliography 204

Introduction

HOW I BEGAN MOVING

By the time I celebrated my fiftieth birthday, I had been living in Orlando, Florida, for twenty years and in Florida for my whole life. In Orlando, I lived less than two hundred miles from my childhood Florida home. Deep down I wanted a change. One day, I listed my life goals based on my current family and job situations. My son was in Scotland attending college, my mother had just died, and the aerospace industry, my employer, was having massive layoffs. The time felt right for a change. One of the goals I listed was, "live in another state." How could that happen? I had never moved alone or even thought about it until now. And indeed, I *was* thinking about it. I began to investigate towns. I began to give away things I didn't really need. I intended to move once and that would be it. So I thought anyway.

I chose Austin, Texas, because my brother lived there and the climate was warm, like Florida. It felt like an easy move for someone who had never moved alone before. The packing, the leaving, and the move went smoothly. But then something unexpected happened. I got homesick—after only six months in Texas! That's when I learned changing places requires a little more than loading up a car and going.

I returned to my home in Orlando, Florida. The next move was closer and part-time. I lived in Gainesville during the week and returned to Orlando on the weekends. Although this solved the homesick problem, it was unsatisfactory because I had not really left home!

Looking back now, I see that these two early attempts to relocate were practice sessions for future successes. They taught me what was involved with moving and strengthened my coping skills. I began to consider locations where I *wanted* to live, not just ones that were easy. Later moves to Anchorage, San Diego, Portland, Denver, San Antonio, and finally back to Austin were successful and rewarding experiences. The delightful details of each move are scattered throughout this book and my rationale for each move is explained in Chapter 9, where moving again is discussed.

Moving to each new town has been richly rewarding for me. Over the course of several moves, I have maintained a house in Florida, doubled my savings, traveled with my adult son, learned the character of many towns, and acquired life-long friends all over the United States. I have been able to reach my life goals of understanding more of America, enjoying many travel adventures, and attending seminary. The fun times have outweighed the lonely times; the discoveries have outweighed the disasters.

> *I regard life*
> *On the whole*
> *As a pretty ordinary affair*
> *Whose main object is to have fun*
> *And find a rare adventure.*
> *– Hawaii*

INTRODUCTION

HOW THIS BOOK IS ORGANIZED

The book is divided into three main parts: *Getting Ready*; *Creating the Right Living Conditions*; and *Seeing How Far You've Come*. The first part, *Getting Ready*, examines your motives and skills for moving. It also contains information about how to decide to move, and once decided, how to make the actual move.

The second part, *Creating the Right Living Conditions*, discusses your life after you've arrived in a new town. The important areas of housing, jobs, practical matters, friends, and feelings are explored. You will discover some surprising choices for housing and jobs as well as some solid advice for making friends and keeping your spirits high.

The last part, *Seeing How Far You've Come*, offers a perspective on all the successes and hard work involved with moving. You will read about the incredible rewards of moving and perhaps even begin to think about a second move.

Even though the information in this book is not offered as legal or financial advice, each chapter offers practical wisdom as well as a personal account of my experiences over the course of eight elective moves. Suggestions, advice, and guidelines are offered for dealing with the important areas of moving in the *Consider This ...* sections. I chose this heading because I expect you, the reader, to choose what is helpful and leave the rest.

In sections called *How I Did It*, I share my own colorful learning experiences.

Each chapter concludes with a brief summary and some questions to get you thinking about you and your next move. Each chapter is independent from the others and you can read in the order of your interests and needs.

xi

UNIQUE PERSPECTIVES OF THIS BOOK

This book has several unique perspectives. Firstly, it was written especially for the single mover. Safety, loneliness, and decision-making can be bigger issues for a single person than they are for a couple or a family. Being single means you must deal with these and other moving challenges alone. Of course, the information in this book can also be valuable for families who are relocating.

Secondly, it was written from the perspective that moving is a choice. It offers suggestions about choosing destinations and about deciding how long to stay. It also recognizes that not everyone has a total choice of destination. The practical advice and experiences I share are helpful whether you are moving by choice or by necessity.

Thirdly, this book assumes no age restrictions. Moving can be a wise choice at any age. You are not too young or too old to consider relocating to a new town. I myself began moving after the Big 5-0.

And lastly, it deals with the subject of multiple moves. If your first move was successful, you may want to try living in another area. Or, if your first move did not meet all your goals, you may want to move again. In either case, subsequent moves will have their own rewards and challenges. And they will be easier than the first one!

HOW THIS BOOK CAME TO BE

When I left Florida for the first time, I did not intend to keep moving. I certainly did not intend to move so much that I could write a book about it! The idea for this book came from a friend in Portland who also wanted to move and asked me how I did it. As I offered my advice she suggested I write a book to share my experiences and my wisdom with others. I listened. A few weeks later I began to get ideas about chapter titles and what I wanted to say in each one. At the same time, I had a mentor who encouraged me to try writing and offered to proofread anything I wrote.

During my weekend solo drives in Oregon, I began to keep pencil and paper handy as I drove. I would hear, "*Say this ...*" "*Tell them that ...*". Finally, I began an outline and made the commitment to write down all I had learned. I had no intention of publishing a book, only getting the information into a form that could be shared with friends and family.

I then began to rewrite the penciled ideas in paragraph form during the gray, rainy days of Portland's winter. Writing this book became a labor of love and tenacity. I tried to write every weekend. After about six weeks of forced writing, the work became fun and I could sit for hours and write. At that time, I was writing in paragraph form in longhand and then typing these notes into a computer file. I wrote in longhand because I found using a computer to compose original text short-circuited my creative processes. I remember one writing session in an empty apartment, where I sat on an inflatable air mattress, writing and wondering when the moving truck would finally arrive. The public radio station was playing *Beethoven's Fifth Symphony*. I had just moved to Denver, Colorado. As I began to compose, I wrote the poem on the following page.

At the seminary school in Denver, I was writing for class assignments and did not enjoy doing personal writing in my spare time. It was only when I settled in San Antonio, and later Austin, that I began to get back the discipline and enjoyment of writing. I changed from writing in longhand to composing on the computer from my handwritten notes. By now, several friends had asked for my information on moving with success. They were ready to move! When would I have my book ready for them? What finally motivated me to complete the project was a commitment to use my experiences to help others move successfully.

The finishing edits were done looking out at palm trees swaying in the trade winds of Honolulu. Yes, I did make my dream move! And after the final edits and move, a terrific publisher appeared who helped me turn the words into a real book!

Although the writing process seemed to never end, it has been a special reward of moving for me. I have discovered my life's purpose and found a new joy in writing that hopefully will translate into writing other books. I hope my stories will amuse you and my information will inspire you to consider changing places.

Ann Cabot
Austin, Texas
June 2005

And here I begin my saga,
Time to write it all down.
From my bowels may the words flow to tell
My story of travel, of new homes,
And of losing the ability to go home.
May I voice the truth,
May I find the words to begin and to end this story
So that I may go on, to the next great chapter of my life.

Part One
GETTING READY

1

Deciding to Go and Deciding Where

CONSIDER THIS ...

Moving. Relocating. What is that? Is it some mysterious black hole where people disappear and are never heard from again? Is it something only the rich and adventurous do? No to both!

Do you have to be crazy to relocate? No again! Moving—relocating—is a healthy, positive experience if you have prepared adequately. This chapter will get you started on that preparation by identifying your motives for moving and the resources you will have available for a move.

For the purpose of this book, moving is defined as the act of relocating your day-to-day activities to another neighborhood, community, town, city, or state for three months or longer. Moving usually implies a long-distance move as from one state to another, or from one coast to the other, but moving can also mean relocating from the city to the suburbs or vice versa.

Moving includes the three-month vacation stay in Hawaii. And the six-month visit to take care of an ailing parent in another town. The critical element of a move is the physical repositioning of your daily existence to another place.

A move can be a voluntary choice. You can choose when and where to move. If you think about it, this means you have limitless possibilities in determining your future. This can be daunting. But don't panic yet! Changing places is not as hard as you may think.

DECIDING TO GO

The first step is deciding to go. This decision can feel like stepping off a cliff. Or it can feel like sprouting wings and flying. In either case, whether terror or exhilaration is your reaction, a decision to move will evoke strong emotions. Let's simplify the decision. The first step is identifying your reasons for wanting to move. The next step is making an honest assessment of your strengths, attitudes, and wealth—resources for the move. These resources will help you thrive during the relocation process. Once you identify these, the butterflies in your stomach (if any exist) will settle down and choosing appropriate locations will become easier. But let's not get ahead of ourselves. What are your reasons for considering a move and what are your resources for making it a success?

A note before proceeding: This book is written especially for those decision-makers who tackle life's big decisions with caution and planning. For those types, the decision to move may be a more extended process. However, if you are an impulsive decision-maker, then you can go directly to *How I Did It* and just enjoy the stories. You are already comfortable with the decision to move.

Knowing Your Reasons and Resources

Why move? This is a very personal question and your answer is important. Moving adds circumstances to your life. What circumstances do you want to add? You get to choose. Some incentives for moving are to experience the adventure of living in an unfamiliar town, to be within a day's drive of friends or family, or for more education. Perhaps you want to live on a boat, in a warmer climate, experience a more ethnically-diverse culture, or exchange city life for a country setting. Are you a widower, empty-nester, or mid-lifer ready for a change, or have you just won the lottery?

> *Don't bloom too early,*
> *That's my advice.*
> *Wait until you're ready.*

Examining why you want to move can also throw new light on your current situation and clarify whether it is satisfactory or not. Maybe you want to move because you are unhappy where you are. Does a new beginning sound really appealing? Or are there particular circumstances you want to change? Your answers can be revealing. They may indicate your proposed move is motivated more by what you want to leave behind than by where you are going. Remember: You take with you all the attitudes, habits, and beliefs you have now. Sage wisdom says if you are relatively happy where you are now, you will be relatively happy in your new location. And the same goes for being unhappy now. Do you believe your happiness or unhappiness is due to your choices and outlooks or to uncontrollable circumstances? The choice to move or not to move can be a first-rate choice if you understand that your happiness is in your control.

It is also important to know what you have for resources, both practical and personal. Resources include not only money but also a support system, good health, and an ability to adapt. These resources are necessary to create the right circumstances for a successful move. What resources do you have?

Time to Count Your Moving Chickens

The following questions are intended to help you assess your own particular situation for moving, to see if you have what it takes to move successfully. Be honest with your answers and you will have a clearer understanding of your ability to move.

1. *Do you enjoy new experiences?*

Do you seek out variety in your daily life? For example, do you enjoy trying new foods or driving on an unfamiliar road? Do you prefer vacationing in a place you've never been before, or in a familiar place? The question of variety is a serious question to think about. A large part of relocating is having a variety of new experiences, some you choose and most you don't. If you enjoy new experiences, then you will more likely enjoy making a move because moving is a huge pot of new experiences, where some of your moving chickens will get tried and fried.

Are others moving with you? Their enjoyment of new experiences must be considered. What is their tolerance for unfamiliar places and new routines? You may enjoy driving a different way to work, but the rest of your gang may prefer the same familiar route. Some of us find life is boring without variety; others find variety to be disruptive.

2. How flexible and adaptable are you?

You may like new experiences but not the surprises that often accompany them. I certainly felt this way when I began moving—I liked change but was not very flexible. What is your tolerance for the unexpected that comes with new experiences? What is your reaction when the unfamiliar road you have dared to take leads to a dead-end and you have to retrace your route? Being flexible will be invaluable during a move because in the beginning, most of what you experience will be unexpected.

3. Are you curious and persistent?

Are you curious about your surroundings and about the people you meet? Are you persistent about maintaining your hobbies and values? These attitudes will work in your favor when you are relocating. They will provide motivation and focus when the frustrations mount up. Being curious will open you to valuable information; being persistent will increase the chances you will get what you want.

If you are a single mover, the information you will need will have to come by your efforts alone. You will have to read the newspaper for activities and you will have to ask strangers for directions. And you will have to go alone to new places and events. Being curious and persistent will be especially helpful resources when you first arrive in a new community.

4. How healthy are you?

Health refers not only to your physical health, but to your mental health as well. (Although some will think you have lost your mental health when you tell them you want to move!) What is your health condition? Do you need the care of a special physician? Is exposure to sun or daylight deprivation a problem? These special health situations must be considered.

Every move is physically taxing. Moving furniture and unpacking boxes will require more exertion and strength than normal activities you have been used to. Are you physically strong enough for this?

Mentally, you will be overloaded as well. Keeping track of finances, dates, and possessions will be mentally taxing. Your brain may rebel. The only glass I ever broke in all my moves was the one I angrily threw into the kitchen sink when I lost the phone number of a new friend in Portland. Do you have tools like organizational skills and relaxation techniques to cope with these situations?

Do you have healthy ways to deal with stress? Eating chocolate doesn't count! Moving is emotionally stressful. You will lose friends, be in unfamiliar surroundings, and be socially isolated. Sleeping and eating routines will be interrupted. How disciplined are you to get the rest, healthy foods, and exercise your body will need to offset feeling overwhelmed, depressed, and fatigued?

Dealing with stress will be discussed more fully in Chapter 6.

5.   *How are your finances?*

Having enough money is important for a successful move. Your goal is to thrive in the new place. Is money available for moving your belongings, making car repairs, leaving apartment and utilities deposits, and all the other expenses that you will incur during a move? Have you saved money for the move? Will you have a reliable income once you move? Will you find a job easily? Will you be able to support yourself, or others, financially after you make this move? Living costs may be lower in the new town or they may be higher. In either case, moving costs money before you arrive in your new community as well as after you move there, so consider this resource and plan wisely.

Other chapters will have valuable suggestions about finances for moving, including Chapter 3 on housing and Chapter 4 on finding a job.

6. *What support system will you have once you move?*

It is important to have a support system as you relocate to a new place, especially if you are a single mover. It may take six months to feel connected to the new community. You will need support during this time of adjustment.

A support system refers to your friends, family, church, or a mentor—anyone who will be at the other end of a phone call, encouraging you and supporting you. Do you have a best friend who says, "Call anytime" and means it? Will you have a counselor or mentor you can contact on a weekly basis? Physicians, accountants, and work associates can also be a part of your support system. The more supporters, the better!

Chapter 5 is devoted to developing a support system in your new community.

7. *Have you had any major changes recently?*

Have you recently had a major life change? These include divorce, job loss, retirement, health changes, death of a loved one, marriage, and a new child. If so, your coping skills may be drained and a move would probably be too stressful at this time. Moving itself is considered a major life change. Consider your timing for the move. Will you be dealing with more than one major life change?

8. Are you optimistic about the move?

What are your expectations for happiness and success after you move? What good fortune do you expect? What unpleasant circumstances do you expect to leave behind? How hard do you think it will be to make friends and become part of a new community? Having realistic, as well as optimistic, expectations will make this move sooooooo much easier. You will adjust more quickly to life the way you find it, and you will be open to events and circumstances far easier than you ever dreamed possible. Realistic and optimistic expectations are a critical element of a successful move.

9. How resourceful are you?

When you run into a challenge, can you find a clever solution? This ability will be a valuable asset during a move. There will be times when circumstances will call for creative solutions and innovative thinking. For example, what would you do if you had forgotten eating utensils on your first day at a new job? This happened to me at Intel, where I was trying to make a good impression on my first day. I had forgotten to bring a fork for my rice-and-beans lunch dish. So, while my food was heating in the microwave, I started looking through the cluttered, abandoned drawers in the kitchen. The only useful thing I found was a pair of chopsticks. At that time, I didn't know how to use chopsticks, but I managed to eat my lunch without staining the expensive white blouse I had worn for my first day. Resourcefulness is essential.

10. How confident are you in your ability to move?

Can you see yourself overcoming dilemmas, finding your way in unfamiliar terrain, and adjusting to a new environment? This attitude is a mark of your confidence to deal with whatever arises during a move. Often, confidence is as important as the ability to deal, because having confidence allows you to try new solutions and experiment in solving the inevitable problems that arise during a move.

Now that you've counted your moving chickens, hopefully you have a clearer understanding of your fitness for making a move and feel confident you have the necessary resources to thrive in a new place. Not yet? That's okay. If you still want to move, you will develop the confidence during the moving process.

Life's Essentials

Here is an exercise that will enhance your understanding of your priorities. It will also help you decide about moving. The exercise is to list what you must have to live the life you want. It sounds obvious, doesn't it? Well, it isn't. Unless you've tried to make this list before, you may find this exercise hard to do. I call the list *Life's Essentials*. To make the list, include no more than twelve items and take time to be sure you have included everything that matters to you.

When I did this for the first time, it took me weeks to sort out what I valued most. Now I use the list to guide many of my choices. For example, one item on my list is *beautiful surroundings*. When I pick apartments to live in, I take special care to choose ones that are attractive and bright. And I spend the extra money to decorate them

> *This is my*
> *Life's Essentials list:*
>
> health
>
> adventure
>
> an amiable relationship
> with son
>
> loyal friends
>
> beautiful surroundings
>
> adequate income
>
> a loving partner

CHOOSE TO MOVE

> **My Son's (age 25)
> Life's Essentials List:**
>
> free lifestyle
>
> interesting friends
>
> good health
>
> abundant income
>
> lots of travel
>
> a job abroad
>
> beautiful furnishings
>
> fun

with color. Another item on my list is *adventure*. I allocate money for trips and take them as often as possible. Without guilt! Over the years since I first did my *Life's Essentials* list, my twelve items have been condensed into seven circumstances that I will not live without. When I move, I make sure that these circumstances are available to me in my new community.

What are your *won't live without* items? Can you recognize how important each is in your life and how each has affected your decisions? Do you have traditional values, like home, or non-traditional values like being unattached? Once you have your *Life's Essentials* list, keep it nearby for a few weeks. Does it make a difference in how you live? Does it confirm your decision to move?

> **Irene's (age 53)
> Life's Essentials List:**
>
> beautiful, comfortable home
>
> safe neighborhood
>
> good relationship with daughter
>
> a husband
>
> enough money to live on
>
> retirement savings

At this point, you should be well on the way to making the first big decision: to move or to stay put. If you have decided that the idea of moving is no longer appealing to you, then you still may want to read the stories of my moving adventures in each *How I Did It* section. The stories will certainly make you laugh. If on the other hand, moving is very appealing, then it's time to begin dealing with some practical issues.

Deciding Where to Go

At this point in the decision-making process, you are ready to consider where to move. Are there locations that you have thought would be appealing places to live? Where are your friends and family living? Remember your reasons for wanting to move in the first place, and be sure those circumstances are available in the communities you are considering. Here are more questions to help you find a location. This is a short set of questions only intended to start the location-choosing process.

1. *What core requirements do you have?*

Regardless of the specific location, every choice should have these basic elements: safety, growing economy, and healthy environment. These are necessary for thriving in the new location. Will all the items you listed for *Life's Essentials* be available in the places you are considering? Are other requirements essential, like closeness to family or year-round recreation? Is weather important and what kind? Is proximity to a large city a requirement? What about demographics? Do you want ethnic diversity or homogeneity? In other words, add other criteria to your *Life's Essentials* list that are location specific to ensure that you are looking for the best place for you! A title for this list might be *"Life's Essentials for Moving."*

2. *What is the cost of living in the new place?*

Pay special attention to the cost of living in the places you are considering. Some places, like Honolulu and New York City, are appealing and also very expensive to live in. These costs will add pressure if you don't get a higher salary to go with them, or if you don't have other sources of income to offset these additional expenses.

CHOOSE TO MOVE

You may relocate to a place with a lower cost of living. In this case, your finances could be enhanced by a move.

3.   Have you researched locations?

Libraries and bookstores have books about almost anyplace you are considering. I used a book called *Places Rated Almanac* to evaluate towns I was considering for relocation. It is published every two years and gives housing costs, crime rates, transportation, weather conditions, schools, and recreational opportunities that are available in each of several hundred metropolitan areas in the United States and Canada.

4.   Will you visit before you move?

If you can visit a place first before moving there, you may have an easier time once you arrive. You will have more realistic expectations of the new community. You will know about the main routes and attractions. You may even find a job and attend local events.

Visiting a place before you move is also a way to jump-start the adjustment process. When you go back home, you can adjust your plans and preparations to be more suitable for the new place. For example, if you discover that your new community rarely gets freezing temperatures, you may decide to leave the wool clothes and velour sofa behind.

5.   How will you and your possessions get transported?

The practical necessity of moving yourself and your belongings has to be considered. Will getting there be an adventure? Will you fly or drive? If you fly, you will need transportation once you arrive. You may need to transport the car you already own. If you drive, you can choose an out of the ordinary, scenic route. A friend may be willing to come along as well. Transporting your belongings is also an important decision. You'll get more information on this later.

Choosing a place to live can be an exciting exercise. You are choosing a new home where you will conduct the important, as well as fun, activities of your daily life: pursuing your hobbies, earning your living, creating social bonds, as well as eating, sleeping, and relaxing. The place you are choosing will be the context for your life and you will be part of its culture. Take your time with this part of the decision-making process and play with your options!

Choice

It is important to remember that everything about this move is a choice. And no matter what the issue, you can always change course if you need to. Every decision has its consequences and trade-offs. You have the choice between moving and staying where you now live. Once you do move, you can choose whether to stay or return. Or you can choose to move on. Once you take one apartment, you can choose to keep it or move out. You can choose this job or that one. Or this friend or that one. Making a choice now does not keep you from changing course later. Knowing that you are free to choose again will, hopefully, allow you to consider a wider range of choices when you move.

Commitment

When you move, it is okay to commit to a little if you don't want to commit to a lot. You can commit to a six-month move if you don't want to think about being gone for three years. You can commit to a month-by-month apartment lease if you don't want to sign up for twelve months. You can commit to reading this book even if you can't commit to moving. It's okay.

CHOOSE TO MOVE

A little commitment is all that is needed to let the adventure take place as it should.

When I move, I usually only commit to a short time at first. When I moved to Oregon, for example, I committed to staying for four months. The dreary winter and lack of friends may have convinced me to move sooner but I had made that commitment. In the end I stayed almost two years and made the best friends I have ever had. But having a long-term commitment was not a prerequisite. When I moved to Denver, I only committed to attend one semester of seminary. Denver's winters were too cold for me and I wanted to live in a warmer climate. Going month-to-month past that first semester, I stayed for almost a year and a half. In all my moves, I never left before my short commitment time and I usually stayed much longer than originally planned.

The World Is as We Are

Have you heard the story of the two newcomers? Each was asked where they came from and how they liked it. The first newcomer replied, "I came from Chickaloon City and I hated it. The weather was too cold, the people unfriendly, and moose ate my vegetable garden."

The second newcomer was asked the same questions. Their reply was, "I came from Chickaloon City and it's an awesome town. We can ski in the winter, people help each other shoveling snow, and the moose hunting is superb."

The point is: Being happy where you are is largely about what you bring with you. If you didn't like your last hometown, you are more likely to dislike a new one. And if you liked the last one, you will probably like this one just fine. When we

DECIDING TO GO AND DECIDING WHERE

I Feel Like the Migrating Salmon

I feel like the migrating salmon
Whose exact birthplace is known,
Whose burial site is watched by visitors from near and far,
But whose whole adult life is spent in an unknown location.

I feel like the great green turtle
Whose plastic eggs are buried (and marked for god's sake!),
Whose return to the nesting grounds is marked on a calendar,
But whose adult life is neither marked by location or activity.
Where do these creatures go and what do they do before they emerge
As full cycled beings?

I am in that uncharted, hidden realm now,
Me in my fifties.
I was on the radar screen when I gave birth,
when I married, when I sent the kid off to college,
And I will again be on the screen when I retire,
put grandchildren to bed, and need bifocals.
But now, this in-between time, this time so ripe with promise,
this last gasp at landing the dreams of my life—
Where am I?

I am surely charting my own course,
As surely as the great-green turtle swims
in kelp in some unknown bay.
I am.
And no name and no passage describes me,
Now that I set my own course, in my own time,
and choose my own labels
To emerge a stronger and truer me than yet realized.

So wait for my return on the shore or in the stream.
I will come again and complete the cycle
Just as it is planned.
I will be known again, but just now, just this time,
I am feasting on the kelp and swimming in the deep waters,
Exploring oceans that no one has told me about before.

Where am I? What are the rules?
All I have are the salmon and the turtles to ask.

CHOOSE TO MOVE

move, we bring with us *all* our baggage, the packed stuff as well as the stuff in our heads.

I learned this slowly as I moved from place to place. I found out home was where I was, not better or worse than before. And I learned that being happy was an inside job and not about my address. If I needed disappointments, I found people and circumstances everywhere to fulfill that need. And if I needed to experience joy, I found that, too. Unfulfilled needs, disappointments, and loneliness are in every town just as there are happy surprises, exciting outings, and incredible friends. What you find in any particular setting is what you go looking for, or perhaps even more so, who you are.

HOW I DID IT

I Feel Like the Migrating Salmon expresses how I felt in the beginning of my moving saga. I had nothing charted, no guidebook, just my desire to move. I will tell you how I made the very first decision to move to a new town in a new state. My decision-making process was so laborious that I still remember it well. I thought it would be a once-in-a-lifetime decision. As it turned out, I made the decision several more times. Let's start with the first time.

My First Move: Orlando, Florida, to Austin, Texas

I was born in Florida in the forties when staying in one place was valued. My early moving experiences were limited to a few moves within the state. For my parents' generation, this would be a suitable, correct thing to do. But for me it was increasingly unsatisfying. I became bored beyond words in

Orlando and the arrival of a world-famous amusement park did not help. I certainly did not want to live my entire life in this one state. My family was gone or far away. My mother had died the year before and my only child was attending college in Scotland. I was ready for a change!

I expected the change to cure all the boredom and to stimulate my interests again. The words of Janet Luhrs, from *The Simple Living Guide,* expressed my feelings at this time: "I love checking out new places, new people, new smells, foods, sensations, new skies, new roads. I love immersing myself in this newness. Traveling is one time I am fully and completely in the moment, fully present like a cat waiting to pounce with all systems go." (p. 403)

There were fears to overcome. The thought of moving to a totally unfamiliar place made me feel wary and scared. And it was hard to give myself permission to make such a big decision based solely on my wants and dreams. And no *Life's Essentials* list existed! I had been fulfilling the roles of mother, daughter, wife, and income producer. So, I took on yet another role, the role of decision-maker, and bought a copy of *Places Rated Almanac.* I studied the statistics for Austin, the city where my brother Paul lived. It offered a strong job market, recreational activities, and low crime. Moving to a place with family was also appealing and my brother welcomed my coming. There were abundant computer jobs and no state income taxes. I liked the size of the city and its warm weather, just like I was used to in Florida. Based on all these aspects, I chose Austin as my new community.

I began to pack my belongings, rent out my house, and find a job in Austin. I thought this would be a permanent move.

(Isn't that what everyone thinks?) I thought I had to take everything that was transportable with me including my dishes, my hedge trimmers (well, you never know), old yard clothes, potted houseplants, and cooking spices, along with the more reasonable items of clothes and art collections.

I wish you could have seen that first move. I stuffed my red sports car, a Datsun 280Z, as full as possible with plants, clothes, aquarium supplies, and art items. I put my bike on the back on a rack. I packed thirty boxes and shipped them to my brother's home. A friend who was helping me remarked, "Ann, do you really need all this stuff?" I thought I did. Today I would never move that much anywhere!

What I did not take with me or mail, I left behind as furnishings for my house that I rented. I put my valuable papers in a safety deposit box. Was I ambivalent about this being permanent? You bet! I forwarded my mail to my brother's address.

The drive to Austin took three days. Each night I took the bike off the rack and put it in the motel room. Each day I peered around palm leaves and fern fronds as I drove. And did I mention the cat? Yes, I moved to Austin with a longhaired white cat. Somewhere in all my belongings she found a cozy corner and napped for most of the trip.

The cat and I and all the possessions made the trip successfully. We moved into my brother's roomy house and I went to work for a small one-man office. I wish I could end the story here, but there is more to tell. In all my planning, what I hadn't considered was the possibility that this move was going to be very hard! I hit an emotional wall during the third month when I realized that I was alone in a new town with few skills for making friends or becoming part of the community. Those were lonely, confusing, humiliating months. My boss turned out to be neurotic and petty, my cat hid under my bed because my brother's dogs chased it, and the warm weather turned into a blistering hot summer. I made SOS calls to my Florida friends often for support. That's when I learned to get really cheap long-distance telephone service. I cried a lot. I expected so much from myself that just wasn't possible in those early days of moving.

After six months of this existence, I repacked the thirty boxes, gave the bike to my brother, found the cat a loving home, left the plants, and drove back to Florida. I didn't plan to move again.

Was my decision wrong? No, neither the one to move nor the one to choose Austin. I had a valid reason to move and had done my research. Was I adequately prepared, emotionally or socially? No. And this made the difference between a successful move and a failed attempt. My later moves, as you will learn, were easier and far more successful.

IN SUMMARY

The decision to move is the first decision you will have to make, and the most pivotal one. A change in residence is one of life's biggest events. Knowing why you are moving, identifying your resources, and deciding where to move are important aspects of the decision to move. Take time to answer the questions in this chapter and determine if moving will benefit your life's goals and dreams. Make this first decision the first right decision! If you decide to move, many other decisions will follow, and this book will help you make them.

CHOOSE TO MOVE

OTHER QUESTIONS TO THINK ABOUT

1. *Where have you always wanted to live? In a big city? In a rural town? By the ocean? Near your grandchildren? On a sailboat?*

2. *What are the pluses and minuses of not moving?*

3. *What benefits do you hope to get from moving to a new place?*

4. *What new experience have you had in the last week? New restaurant? New route from work? New movie? New food taste?*

5. *Name three towns or cities you think may be appealing to live in.*

2

Leaving

CONSIDER THIS ...

Leaving is what happens on the outside once the decision to move has happened on the inside. It is about closing doors in order to open new ones. Leaving requires a willingness to reach beyond the present to potential that lies in the future and in a new place. Leaving involves accounting for the possessions that form your physical world as well as redefining the personal and business affiliations that constitute your social world. Leaving is sad work, hard work. It requires important decisions to be made. It creates loss because you will not maintain the same friends, belongings, or lifestyle that you have now.

> *I'm leaving with an armful of yellow daylilies*
> *High hopes and a life;*
> *I've had a lot of suns shining on me.*
> *I'm taking red apples and red rhubarb*
> *Green zucchini and golden sunflowers*
> *And big, bulging bags of memories—*
> *I'm going to paint a sunrise.*

And it requires making decisions about moving the things you own. One decision for each!

To help you anticipate both the losses and the decisions, this chapter will treat the subject of leaving in terms of what is being left: personal belongings, residence, friends, family, and business. It will discuss sorting, packing, and moving possessions; leaving your residence (either owned or rented); and redefining relationships with friends and family. It will also examine how to move your vehicle and identify business contacts that may need to be replaced in the new community.

Personal Belongings: Keepers or Leavers?

I dearly love my possessions, although I have fewer of them these days. I derive a certain identity and security from having my mother's cedar chest, the chair I bought in Costa Rica, and the art from Alaska. Happiness? Well, I don't know. I only know it feels satisfying to share space with my things. So satisfying that I will spend the time and energy to carefully pack them, lift them onto a truck, drive them to the next destination, and celebrate with them at another adventure's doorstep.

How many possessions do you need to be happy? Or secure? Or content? However much it is, it will always be a little or a lot more than you really need. And it will never be zero. Even the woman traveler whom I met in Glacier National Park had big pockets in her coat. No camera like me, no gifts, no souvenirs, no snacks, and no extra suitcase ... but still something in those pockets. Possessions are artifacts of our existence. Our responsibility is to be conscientious of the choices we make about them.

What do personal belongings do for us? They give us a sense of identity and history, since they provide a certain connection to our past. A piece of art recalls an extraordinary trip to the Arctic, or Mother's needlepoint pillow reminds me I had a loving mother long after she has gone. Familiar possessions can make a new apartment feel like home. Sleeping on your favorite Egyptian cotton sheets somehow wards off the night's anxieties. Personal belongings can provide color, comfort, and identity in the new community.

So, how much of what you own do you want to move? Don't just pack up everything. Think about where you are going and what lifestyle you will have. If you are going to rent an apartment, you won't need the wheelbarrow and shovel. If you are moving to Florida from Minnesota, you won't need the parkas and wool hats. On the other hand, if you are moving to Florida but want to vacation in the Arctic, bringing warm clothes along may be a wise idea. The appropriateness and usefulness of each item are important considerations. How much space will you have available at your new place? If you are moving from a large place to a smaller place, there may not be room for the king-sized bed or the full-length sofa. You may have to store or sell the larger items and buy smaller ones to replace them. Double or twin-sized bedding moves easier and fits better in a smaller place. A love seat and a stylish chair substitute well for a full-sized sofa.

In addition to considering the usefulness of your possessions and how much room you'll have at the other end, think about whether you plan to move back; how long you will be gone; how much you can afford in moving costs; how replaceable the items are; and your gut feelings of attachment to each of your personal belongings. Often attachment wins out over practicality. That's just fine. This is your move to do the way

CHOOSE TO MOVE

you want. Actually, deciding about your personal belongings is quite simple. Two choices are available to you: keep them or shed them. Keeping personal belongings can mean moving them with you or storing them locally. Shedding personal belongings can be done by selling them or donating them. Let's look at each alternative.

Storage

If you decide to keep the lawn chairs, the Oriental rug you got at a bargain price, and the afghan your grandmother stitched for you, then you have another decision to make. You can take personal items with you or store them before you leave. Public storage units abound these days and they are glad to take your money in exchange for storing your belongings. Both climate-controlled and natural storage units are available in several sizes. How you arrange your belongings in the unit is important. Put the heavier, more solid boxes on the bottom. Especially with natural units, leave a space between the floor and your items to allow air to circulate. You will be required to supply your own lock. Ask about the security measures of the complex and notice the attention to security given by the

> ### *Poem to a Storage Unit in Denver*
>
> *King Tut's tomb*
> *In the side of a hill,*
> *I choose you to house my finest treasures*
> *While I am away in a far country*
> *Exploring.*
>
> *Keep them cool, keep them dry, and*
> *Decorate your walls with them if you must.*
> *I will return after awhile*
> *And empty you of my precious treasures*
> *And will thank you.*
>
> ❦

26

attendants on duty. It should have a gated entry and daytime attendants. Generally, storage units that are in less convenient locations and ones that are not climate-controlled are less expensive to rent. You can pay the rental charge by the month, quarter, or year. Often, if you choose to pay by the quarter or year the owners will send you a notice of the rent due. That is very convenient and remedies the "out of sight, out of mind" problem of forgetting to pay the rent on time.

Remember, there are no guarantees offered by any storage unit complex for the safety of your belongings. Have you considered the risks? Especially if items are not stored in a climate-controlled unit, they could be exposed to termites, mold, or excessive heat. They could get stolen if security is not enforced. The wise course is to store only what you could live without if the worst case happens. And buy insurance. Being paid for any loss will help a little. Some public storage facilities may be able to arrange for a rental truck when the time comes to move out.

Transporting

You may choose to take most of your personal possessions with you to your new residence. How do you move them? Certainly the cost is a big piece to consider in this decision. The cost is partially determined by the amount you have to move. It is also determined by the method you choose for transportation. Renting a U-Haul trailer or truck will be less expensive than hiring a professional moving company. Who will drive and what about your personal vehicle? Do you tow it behind? The loading and unloading can be done by you and your friends or by a hired crew.

A more expensive choice is to hire a professional mover. Their price will depend on the total weight of your furnishings. When I chose a mover to move me to Denver, I was curious about their weight estimate. So, I drove with the moving van to the scales to see if the estimates were correct. This is an interesting exercise and I suggest you do it. Besides the actual transport, the effort and cost of packing has to be considered. Packing your personal belongings yourself will be less expensive than having a mover pack them. Do you have the time? For boxed items, shipping by regular mail will be less expensive than using a shipping service.

Also consider the safety of your possessions during the move. Could there be loss or damage? Are you moving valuable heirlooms that need extra protection? If you are a careful packer—wrapping and padding *every* piece—your personal belongings will probably arrive undamaged. If you load them yourself and drive them yourself, you will be assured of the treatment they will receive. Although professional movers are usually very reliable, you never can be sure how much your belongings are handled. Sometimes they will be loaded and unloaded several times before they reach your new home. If you are worried, do as much yourself as you can. I only used a mover once and was dismayed at the driver's unconcerned attitude over several crushed boxes. And honestly, I hated to be away from my belongings. If ever there was a time to feel homeless, it will be when that huge moving truck slowly crawls out of your driveway with most of your earthly belongings stacked inside. Waiting for it to arrive at the other end can feel like an eternity! For these reasons, I drove my own things for all the other moves. Yes, I am overly protective when it comes to my personal belongings.

LEAVING

Packing

Once you decide what to keep and what to leave behind, packing is the next big order of business. This can be an overwhelming task. I would suggest doing the packing in stages. Pack items you are not currently using. These might include seasonal yard equipment or travel gear that won't be used before the move. Or you could begin to pack by moving the items you plan to leave in storage. This will also make room to sort through possessions and pack them.

Another scheme to make packing more manageable is to pack one room at a time. Perhaps pack one room a week. Or one closet every weekend. Granted, you don't get a master plan out of this; that is, you may not pack all your books in the same box. But it will accomplish the packing in smaller chunks and let you see progress throughout the huge task. A word of encouragement: The extra care you take with packing breakable items will pay off when you unpack them still in one piece. As you seal each box, remember to label its contents and the room where it goes, if you know.

My Beloved Belongings

My beloved belongings are all locked in boxes.
Packed.
I hate it.
Red Mexican pots,
White down coverlet,
Black whales on an aqua canvas.
These are sources of my pleasure and my passion,
And now they are all locked away unseen.
Soon ... I hope ... I will arrive in town and
Free them to play within the spaces of my daily life.

CHOOSE TO MOVE

Selling

You've decided not to keep some of your possessions. What do you do with them? The American way is to have a garage sale and distribute the wealth. The money you get may be minimal but the goodwill the sale will create in your neighborhood will be worth the effort. Don't be greedy with your prices and do mark them on the items. Follow the community rules for garage sales and tell your neighbors. Advertising the sale in the local newspaper depends on how much you have to sell. Furniture and children's things are strong draws and advertising those items may be worthwhile. Larger items, like appliances, also may warrant advertising. If there is a business nearby that has a bulletin board, post an eye-catching notice. Plan to spend several days putting price tags on items plus one or two days attending the sale. If you have a lot of items to sell, get a friend to come help. The friend will also keep you company. Sitting with the things that you bought, loved, moved from room to room, and now are leaving behind can be a sad time. It's not a good time to be alone.

Donations

Suppose you don't want to invest the time and effort (and possibly emotions) to sell your leftovers. Another way to dispose of them is to donate them to a worthy cause. Thrift shops for Hospice, spouse abuse centers, and religious organizations are in every town in America. Youth programs have their own garage sales and Goodwill Donation Centers take what you no longer need. Making a charitable donation is not so much about getting a tax credit as it is about helping someone else have an improved quality of life. If you do want to get a tax credit, be sure you get a receipt for the donation.

30

Clothing

A special note about clothes. Styles are different in different cities. This has as much to do with the weather as it does with the culture. My flannel shirts from Anchorage were worn half as much in Oregon and not at all in Texas where air-conditioning was mandatory. I carried a handmade pair of leather sandals with me to Anchorage, Portland, and Denver until I was able to wear them in warmer climates or on vacation. As soon as I arrived in Austin I wore them summer and winter. In Denver, my tank tops and shorts stayed in a suitcase while in Austin, my wool blazer and down jacket never saw the light of day.

Colors are also place specific. Darker colors were the style in Portland, especially cranberry, forest green, and black. In Austin, those colors are not comfortable to wear and bright Mexican colors like mustard yellow and turquoise are more popular. My advice is to prune your wardrobe before you relocate. It's a chance to justify parting with all the clothes you haven't enjoyed wearing. You'll find replacements for them that suit the new location and new climate much better.

Valuables

How have you kept your most valuable possessions? These could be heirloom jewelry, coin collections, or important documents like wills or house abstracts. Having them in a safety deposit box is convenient and safe. If you have a safety deposit box, should you keep it? If you are thinking of moving back, keeping it is an excellent idea. The rent can be paid by mail. On the other hand, taking your valuables with you may be more sensible and more convenient. If you aren't sure, you could plan to keep the safety deposit box with its contents for six months and then decide. Remember, for any decision, another decision can be made later.

Sorting the Memories

Moving requires you to sort your personal belongings as well as any stored possessions from the past. Up to now, it has been easy to shut away articles from the past by storing them in some faraway closet. It may be difficult to revisit the treasures you have had packed away for a long time. They may be family heirlooms, toys of now-grown children, or furniture from a marriage that no longer exists. The past comes alive just when the future is trying to make its space in your life. Decisions about keeping these treasures can be difficult. Memories can be intense. Feelings of sadness, regret, longing, or happiness may flood your consciousness. They come on top of an overflow of feelings and emotions from the pending move itself.

This is a time when rituals can help. You could perform a ritual such as lighting a candle or burning some token of the past. In this way you signify a change from the past to the bright and hopeful future you have chosen for yourself. Have a support system of friends as you go through this sorting-out time. Get plenty of rest and take breaks of relaxation and fun whenever possible. These will equip you to better deal with the emotions that inevitably come as you sort through the memories.

Can't Decide?

What if you aren't sure about whether to keep or give away a personal treasure? With one exception, my advice is to keep an item if you are at all in doubt about parting with it. Nothing is worse than lying awake at night obsessing on something you gave away but wish you had kept. It becomes like the mosquito in the dark that won't leave you alone. Remember what was said in the first chapter—for every decision, you can always decide again. In this case, keeping the object gives you the option to decide later to let it go.

The exception to this advice is for something that was given to you by someone who treated you badly, or for things that remind you of an unpleasant time in your life. In these cases, keeping the possessions will only keep negative energy and negative memories in your life. Letting go of people and events from the past involves letting go of the material possessions associated with them. Have the vision for your new location filled with treasures not yet seen, treasures with happy memories and friendly people connected to them. Let go of the negative stuff.

HOUSE: RENT, SELL, OR MAINTAIN?

Leaving your house or apartment—your familiar living space—can be a huge lunge or a small step. It can involve leaving a home full of twenty years' worth of memories or it can be as easy as writing a letter of intent to vacate, depending on how deeply rooted you are. If you rent, moving will be easier than if you own a home. Moving from a rented space is more about moving your possessions, discussed in the section above. When you own a house, leaving can consume your emotions, energy, and time. Because it can be so involved, I will focus this section on moving from a house you own.

Leaving your owned residence may trigger serious emotions. You may feel a loss of security (illusion though it may be) when you leave your safe shelter behind. There may be a loss of belonging to a familiar place. Doubtless you will be going to another safe shelter, but it is hard to feel you belong there beforehand. Within the walls of your home are the reminders of who you are and of events from the past. When you leave these walls, you cannot imagine how the new housing will feel or how it will look. During the packing and for the first few months in your new home, you may feel like you do not have a home. This sense of homelessness is not pleasant for most of us.

Fears and sadness are dominant feelings at this stage of moving. I certainly experienced these feelings each time I moved from one home to another. Having someone you can share these emotions with helps you deal with them and move on. Getting enough rest and healthy, nutritious food lessens the chance of your getting too tired or sad. Having fun once in awhile, even if it means leaving other tasks until later, is a wise choice. Go to an entertaining movie, splurge on an ice cream sundae, or try a new hiking path. You will return with renewed energy and a new outlook on your future. Moving can be in your best interest even if right now it feels overwhelming and you feel miserable.

In addition to the emotional impact of leaving your house, you will have the big decision to make of what to do with it. You will have to decide whether to sell, rent, or otherwise maintain your house while you are away. Each choice has its benefits as well as its drawbacks. Now we'll take a closer look at the pros and cons of each option.

Renting

If you decide to rent your house, you are inviting strangers to live in your home. What will happen to the walls and floors and appliances when other people use them? Hope for the best but be prepared for the worst-case scenario. Carpets may get stained, rents may be delinquent, and your precious herb garden may go unwatered. If you rent your house furnished, can you afford to part with the furniture? It may be ruined or stolen. I had one set of tenants who moved all my furniture to the garage, where a leak from the air-conditioner unit produced water stains that made sofas and mattresses unusable. It was the last time I rented my house furnished!

The outside of the house needs care as well. The grass will need cutting and the trees will need maintenance. Don't assume your renter will do it. One solution is to make arrangements for a local yard service to cut the lawn and prune the trees on a regular basis. This will be a monthly expense, but the chances are good that a business will more reliably care for your yard than renters would. You can increase the rent to cover that expense.

Once a renter moves out, the process begins all over again. Your house must be readied for the next renters. Walls may need painting, carpets may need cleaning, and trash may need removing. New renters need to be found. If you have the time and live nearby, you can do these things yourself. Otherwise, you will need help. This is where a rental agency or a property manager can help. They have services that range from securing and qualifying renters to hiring painters and repairmen for maintenance. The best way to find a reliable rental agency is to get recommendations from friends and then interview the prospective agent. Fees vary according to the services you hire them to do.

What about insurance and taxes? Your homeowner's insurance will change to renter-occupied status to insure only the house structure and not the belongings inside. This type of insurance policy usually costs less than a homeowners' policy. Taxes will change, too. The IRS considers rent payments to be ordinary income. All maintenance costs, rental management costs, insurance, and improvements to the house often can be deducted from the total rental income to compute actual taxable income. The federal tax calculations are more complicated for the initial year of renting your house, but after that they are fairly easy. It may be a wise idea to have your tax returns prepared by a professional for the first year that your house is used as rental property.

Retaining your primary residence may have other tax advantages. Some professions pay per diem expenses if the worker has a permanent address in another state. These expenses are paid because it is assumed you are working a temporary assignment away from your permanent residence. These expenses are not taxable by the federal government for up to one year. Having a primary residence elsewhere can be an attractive tax advantage for a year.

If you can live with the downside scenarios described, and if the rents are high in your area, then renting may be a better option for you. Your chances of renting your house are favorable in most places in the country. And you will probably be able to cover any mortgage payments with the rental income. To check the rental market in your area, call a reputable realtor that deals with rental properties.

Renting your house could provide additional income as well as enable you to still own it, but it also requires your time and attention to find a reliable renter and answer calls for leaky faucets and jammed disposal units. Renters may damage your house. When deciding whether to sell or keep your house, it is important to consider your financial situation. Will you be able to afford making two housing payments if no renters come knocking?

Another consideration is the health of the housing and rental markets where you live. How fast are the houses appreciating in your area? Is this an advantageous time to sell? If the housing market is strong, perhaps your house has increased in value and can be sold for a good profit. However, if the rental market is strong, you could ask for and get higher rent payments.

Selling

Most people sell their houses when they move. It is often the easiest way to have the cash to reinvest in a new location. Sometimes the sales proceeds from a house are what finance the move in the first place! If you sell your house yourself, you will avoid paying a commission to a real estate agent. On the other hand, a professional agent can handle the day-to-day work of screening applicants and showing your house, as well as completing the sales contract and calculating expenses. They earn their commission!

There are also prudent reasons not to sell. The house you own can be an investment and the longer you own it, the more it is worth, in most cases. Weigh this against the immediate cash gains from selling. Also consider what other investments you could make with the money from the sale.

Would you ever want to move back to your house? After you are away and living in a strange, new neighborhood, your old hometown may look really appealing. You may value the

CHOOSE TO MOVE

familiar neighborhood and the house with the memories more than you did at the beginning of a move. Don't be in a hurry to sell. Weigh the long view, too. If you have a choice, sell only when you are ready to sell. Remember, I took six years to decide to sell my own house.

Maintaining

If you decide not to rent and are not ready to sell your house, you still have several options for maintaining it while you are away. One option is to lock the front door and let it remain empty. This may look easy but there are drawbacks. The outside appearance has to be maintained while you are away. If your house is unoccupied, who will let you know when your yard begins to look like a jungle? Water pipes could leak, vandalism could occur, or neighborhood children could take up residence in your trees. For example, my tenant found a twelve-inch-long yellow jacket nest thriving in the soil of my rental house in Florida. From halfway across the country, I found an exterminator to remedy the problem, but it wasn't easy. Letting a house remain empty usually isn't a wise choice. Houses are better taken care of when they are lived in.

Another option for keeping the house relatively empty is to hire a house sitter. This could be a wise choice if you are sure you will be returning to live in the house within a few months. A house sitter may have their own furnishings in case you leave the house unfurnished. This person could be an acquaintance or a professional house sitter. In either case, someone will be living in your house and taking care of it, and you may be paying *them*. Hire someone with references or who is well known to you, someone you can trust. They will be responsible for the safety and security of your residence while you are away. You will have to decide whether this is a wise and cost-effective option for your circumstances.

Neighbors can be very helpful at this time if you decide to maintain your house while you are away. They can notify you of changes to the house or neighborhood. Remember to include them in your travel narratives and call to keep in touch. They will miss you just as much as you will miss them. Usually they will be glad to help and delighted to know you are succeeding in your new community.

What will *you* do about *your* house? Now that you have an idea of decisions to be made and the options available to you, you can make informed choices about this very important aspect of moving.

Vehicle: Keep or Sell?

How will you move your personal vehicle? Driving is an obvious choice. If you are driving your personal vehicle to the new location, you can fill it with your special belongings. These may include breakable, valuable, or irreplaceable items you don't want to lose. Have a plan for what to do at night when you stop for rest, both for your own safety and for the safety of belongings you carry in the vehicle. Will you take things into the motel room with you, or will you have them cleverly hidden in the car? If you decide to drive, go see friends who live along the way. If done the right way, getting to your new community can be a mini-vacation. You will certainly need one after preparing for this move!

If you decide not to drive your vehicle, shippers will deliver it right to your new front door. I have used this method and

39

found it very satisfactory. Shipping your vehicle usually takes several weeks and you will have to make other arrangements for transportation until it arrives.

You can also sell your vehicle. Depending on its age and condition, you may not want to move it. If you have lived in conditions like salted roads or high humidity, your vehicle may tend to rust more and you may not want to move it. If you decide to sell, you don't have to replace it right away, especially if your new community has convenient public transportation. You would actually be doing the environment a favor to ride the bus. If you do decide to buy another vehicle right away, be aware this could add stress or, if you are lucky, it could be a wonderful addition to a new beginning.

LEAVING FRIENDS

According to most people, your friends are your most valuable possessions. They sustain you, they amuse you, and they enrich you. How do you leave them? How *can* you leave them? Certainly not without sadness and probably not without tears. Have a ceremony, perhaps in the form of a party, to acknowledge this pending separation. It can be an occasion to remember the fun times and to say good-bye. It may help to close the past with blessings and forgiveness. A ceremony gives your friends a chance to wish you well on your new adventure. And it gives you the chance to share your hopes and dreams for the new place.

Take heart. You will not lose all your friends when you move. Some will be able to keep in touch despite the lack of day-to-day contact. For these friends, your leaving will not end the friendship but will embellish it. Treat yourself to an attractive address book and record your friends' addresses, including physical and e-mail, with phone numbers, including area codes. Then as you make the move, keep in touch with them. Buy postcards on the road if you drive to your new town. Tell them what the countryside looks like or what new foods you are eating. After you arrive in your new hometown, send postcards with pictures of your new town so your friends can share your experiences. Go exploring and take photos. Send

Pizza on Paper Towels: Reflections of a Move

I am having another floor party,
Sitting with my Austin friends
On my cleaned floor
And eating pizza on paper towels.
All my chairs are stacked in the storage unit,
All my dishes are cushioned with cardboard and boxed.
For this move my car has been sold
And driven away just an hour ago.

On the floor
We are having a celebration
Of my move and of my life.
Privately, inwardly, I remember having done this before
And feel the sadness and gratitude now
As I felt then.
My life has become a string of moves,
Connected to each other by interstates and floor parties.

I am thankful for my friends here and from the past,
Eating pizza on paper towels
And bidding me farewell.
When I'm ready, I'll put a clasp on my string of moves
And retire to some lovely hillside with my memories
Of pizza on paper towels.

CHOOSE TO MOVE

some of the duplicate copies back to your friends. The bottom line is: Don't wait until Christmas to share your move.

I was surprised how many visitors I had by making the effort to stay in touch. Every time I have moved, I have had two or three visits from friends from my previous hometown because they wanted to share the fun and places I had written to them about. Visits from friends helped during the initial adjustment time when I was sure I would never have another friend in my life!

Some friendships cannot survive the loss of day-to-day contact. Some friends will not remain in your life after you move. These friends may include the people you work with or those you see on a regular basis. The ties of these friendships may not be strong to begin with, or perhaps the friendship was focused on doing things together. Once the activity ceases, so will the friendship. For those, you will have to grieve the loss and move on emotionally. Remind yourself that you will find new friends who will share hobbies and take weekend hikes with you. For now, just accept that friendships will be lost and replaced.

LEAVING FAMILY

Leaving family can be the hardest part of bidding good-bye to a place. I don't know why that is, but I suspect it is about change and about loss and about growing up. I know when I decided to move away from Austin and leave my brother, he was very disappointed. He supported me but he knew we wouldn't be seeing each other as often or share as much. And when my adult son wanted to move, I forgot about the exciting adventures he would experience and instead worried about never seeing him. Leaving family members is a highly charged and emotionally stressful process. The leaving may not be the neatest cut, but the wounds usually heal and support finally comes.

If you are lucky enough to have a supportive family that celebrates your growth and adventurous spirit, then your move will be so much easier. Tell them your plans and progress along the way. Get their ideas and accept the help you need. They may even assist with packing and forwarding mail after you are gone. In any case, having a formal celebration with family members will help move the leaving process along. Staging an event and serving food is a fun way for all to feel included in the move. You can discuss plans, laugh at problems, and anticipate future visits.

Part of your family structure may be a pet. Dogs, and cats especially, don't like a change in their routine or living space. Moving for them can be very difficult. You will have to be sure their health and safety needs are taken into consideration. Transporting a pet can be a challenge, although less of one now than in the past. Now companies transport pets in comfort and safety, even to a foreign country. I knew a couple that moved to France from Texas. They hired a company to fly their two pedigreed dogs in a pressurized cabin, and they were delivered to the new residence in happy spirits and good health.

If you want to take your pet with you on the road, be sure it is accustomed to riding in a car. You have enough responsibilities without having a frightened, carsick pet. No matter what method you choose, I doubt having a pet makes moving any easier. It can, however, make the move feel more like an adventure—one you can share.

CHOOSE TO MOVE

LEAVING PROFESSIONAL AND PERSONAL SERVICES

The professional and personal services you use now will change when you move. These services include business services such as banking, insurance, accounting, and brokerage. Most of these services will have to be re-established in your new community. One exception is your bank. You don't really have to change your bank anymore. Banking long-distance has become easier in today's banking environment where a bankcard can extract money from an account in all but the smallest towns. (I do remember once visiting a town in central Georgia and not being able to use my bankcard to get cash anywhere in the town. I had to drive to the next largest town, some thirty miles away, to the one automatic teller machine. But this is the exception, not the rule.)

If you decide to open a new account in the new community, look for banks offering accounts with no monthly charges. Banks try to attract new customers by offering free checking accounts. Check the local newspaper. If you are considering moving again in a year or two, look for banks that have branches throughout the country. I recently opened an account with Bank of America because they are so widespread. It's not a guarantee though. In Anchorage, the Bank of America was bought out by Northrim Bank. I do not recommend keeping both the old account and the new account. The bookkeeping can just get too complicated.

For insurance, there are advantages and disadvantages to transferring policies to your new town. It is usually cheaper to carry car insurance in the state where you live. I found this out when I insured a truck in Florida, then moved to Alaska and kept the Florida insurance. Later I learned rates were lower in

44

Alaska for that vehicle. An unusual twist to this story happened when the front windshield was cracked by a flying rock. In the Florida coverage, the windshield got replaced for free. If I had carried the Alaskan equivalent insurance, I would have paid to have it replaced. This story illustrates that advantages and disadvantages vary with the locations involved.

For accounting services and brokerage services, long-distance business is possible, but I don't recommend it. Accountants are more familiar with taxes for the state in which they do business. Hiring a Texas accountant to do Colorado taxes may be asking for trouble. So, plan to find a local accountant.

Stockbrokers have a different problem. They must be licensed in the state where their client lives. If you want to keep your personal broker after you move to a new state, they may have to pay for an additional license. Also, you will no longer be able to meet with them face to face; this can be unsatisfactory when you are talking about investing your dear money. Local stockbrokers are a more satisfactory arrangement.

The services of physicians, alternative medicine practitioners, and dentists need to be established locally as well. As much as you would like to, you cannot bring your family doctor with you. But you can ask your hometown doctor or dentist for references in your new community. They have access to professional organizations with member listings and may find a colleague in your new town. You can also ask for recommendations from coworkers or others in your new community. It may take time and several visits to find satisfactory medical services.

Your goal should be to feel comfortable, on a professional and personal level, with the physicians, dentists, and other

CHOOSE TO MOVE

health workers you choose to care for you. This extends to your chiropractor, massage therapist, and physical trainer. You may have to choose again in your search for suitable medical services. When I was in Portland, I tried three dentists before I felt at ease with one. When I was in Austin, I found a likeable physician quickly. Both discoveries were from recommendations of coworkers.

Neither will you be able to take folks who provide personal services with you. These include car mechanics, personal hairdressers, seamstresses, and pet groomers. No, you can't send the dress to be hemmed through the mail! For some of us, the loss of these supporters is major. I never feel secure in a new town until I have found a qualified mechanic and a talented seamstress. These personal services make our lives so much easier.

In your search for excellent mechanics or hairdressers, ask for recommendations. This is the quickest way to find what you need. Finding satisfactory personal services is a matter of trial and error. Don't get discouraged! You deserve to be pampered.

LEAVING FAMILIAR THINGS

Most of us are creatures of habit, going and doing in the same, familiar ways. Some of these familiar habits include regularly-watched TV shows, favorite foods, and familiar routines. These give life structure and comfort. They add a sense of the familiar that makes life feel safe. Usually you don't even think about them. But when you move, these favorites may no longer be available to you and you may have to deliberately build new habits.

46

For example, favorite TV shows may not be shown in the new community, or at the same time. One of my favorite TV shows, *Charlie Rose*, was shown in Portland and Denver. Watching Charlie and his guests became part of my end-of-the-day routine. But the show didn't air in Texas. Months went by and I developed other ways to end my day. Then one night I turned on the TV and there he was, black background and all. I was ecstatic! I had found a familiar friend again.

Do you have shows you watch on a regular basis? How much would you miss them if they weren't available? If you are twitching, this is important.

I also have preferred foods. They include tangy peperoncini peppers, Oregon strawberry-rhubarb jam, lemon-dill mustard, and ginger beer. In a new town, I scan the shelves of grocery stores for these food favorites. Make a list of your favorite foods. You may not have access to them in your new hometown. But with any luck, you will find outstanding replacements. Remember those peperoncini peppers I liked? Well, I discovered them in Anchorage when I could not find other favorite peppers. When I become really desperate, I have a friend send a care package of my favorite foods. You can do that, too. Your friends will understand.

Familiar routines may be altered by your move as well. What are the activities you make a point to do on a regular basis? Do you take your pet to a special dog park every afternoon? Do you swim across the same bay twice a week? Can you snorkel at a beach that is nearby? Will you be able to keep these routines or activities in your new community? Do you even want to? Routines and activities give our lives structure and enjoyment. Decide the ones you want to continue

CHOOSE TO MOVE

after you move or what new routines you want to establish. Deliberately planning and scripting your life is part of creating the right circumstances for a successful move.

HOW I DID IT

A line from a poem goes, "what cannot be untied has to be cut." In leaving, sometimes I untied and sometimes I cut. In either case, I experienced sadness and loneliness for what I was leaving. Later, I felt excitement about having new possessions, friends, and routines in my life. Leaving has gotten easier for me because I have known what to expect. For me, personal belongings, friends, and family have been the most important and hardest things I have left. Some of them I have left more than once.

Leaving My Home and Belongings

The first time I totally severed ties with my personal belongings occurred when I moved to Anchorage, Alaska. I still owned my house and arranged to have friends stay in my home until I decided how long I would be away. This was more satisfactory than renting to strangers and gave me a place to stay when I came to visit. I stored valuable possessions like an antique rocking chair and family photo albums in a locked closet. I left my art on the walls and let the house sitters use the yard tools in exchange for mowing the grass and trimming the bushes. They took excellent care of my home.

I maintained my original bank account at a credit union and opened another checking account in Anchorage. I kept my local mailbox but had the mail forwarded to Anchorage because I did not know how soon the snow, ice, and darkness would send me running back home to Florida.

I did not move furnishings because Anchorage was too far away and I had rented my house furnished. I leased a one-bedroom empty apartment, then went to Wal-Mart and bought an inflatable mattress, a lawn chair, and a card table. I was in business! I also discovered a wonderful side of Anchorage—yard sales happen all summer long. Every telephone pole is covered with sale notices and every neighborhood has its corners crowded with cardboard signs on wooden poles pointing the way to a sale.

From these sales I bought a pair of snow boots for a dollar, a set of skis for five dollars, a comforter for three dollars, assorted pans, dishes, and glasses, as well as an answering machine, and a TV set. Evidently, Anchorage is the end of the road for merchandise. Since it can go no further north, it just gets sold and resold every summer! Several sellers told me they were heading south after getting tired of the cold and darkness. They surely didn't want to pay a second time to take home things they had paid dearly to bring with them!

I stayed in Anchorage almost a year and then moved to San Diego. By this time, I had been away from my house in Florida for a year and had rented it to strangers. They had, in turn, rented it to their in-laws who promptly moved all the furniture into the garage, where sofas, chairs, beds, and boxes collected mold and spider webs. Then the air conditioner leaked water into the garage and onto the furniture. I returned to find a sad mess with not much to salvage. I had a huge garage sale. What didn't sell went to Goodwill. One morning in the warm Florida sun, two mattresses, a dining table, a sofa, and a bed frame sat

CHOOSE TO MOVE

forlornly in my driveway waiting to be hauled away. My best friend came over to share the moment and we remembered all the confidential chats on that sofa.

Remember the closet I had locked with my personal belongings? The renters picked the lock and helped themselves. Now, years later, it is just a memory. But at the time I felt abused and vulnerable. Later, other renters were excellent tenants, staying for long periods of time, and caring for the house as I would have.

The next major move was to Portland, Oregon. It was more permanent. I knew I could handle the logistics of moving, so I decided to take all my possessions with me. I packed my paintings and artwork carefully into boxes and taped them tightly. I bought a smaller sofa, the love-seat variety, and a new double-sized mattress. I packed them in a U-Haul for the long drive to Portland. Eric, my son, flew down from Anchorage to drive with me across the United States from Florida through Georgia, Arkansas, Colorado, over the Rocky Mountains, through Utah and Idaho, and finally along the Columbia River Gorge to Oregon. Experiencing the Great Plains for the first time was wonderful. The flatness of the wheat fields created wide vistas and the gray snow clouds added drama. Although we started the trip on December 27, we encountered surprisingly little snow. Remember my advice about having a mini-vacation? Well, we took that truck on dirt roads to see waterfalls and parked it with other tourist vehicles at overlooks in Idaho. We had fun despite the hard work of moving.

In Portland, I rented a much smaller space than my Florida house. I wanted my possessions unboxed and usable because I had been without them for almost a year. It was exquisite

50

to be living among them again! I hung all my artwork—over fifty pieces, many sharing the same wall—and displayed my Alaskan ivory carvings. Across the kitchen cabinets I placed carved wooden birds from my collection. It was home at last! I left the safety deposit box in Florida, emptied the house of all its furnishings, and opened a bank account in Portland where I could have my paychecks deposited directly.

I did not want to take my high school yearbook, picture albums, an antique spinning wheel, or a set of deer antlers from my father to Portland. Instead, I stored them and other unneeded things in a storage rental unit, where they stayed for over four years. I have often wondered whether these belongings were worth all the money I spent on rent!

My red Datsun 280Z was transported on a commercial truck to San Diego and then I drove it to Oregon. The car was fifteen years old and the trip to California would have been hard on it. It did get to see Death Valley, Mt. Shasta, and the Pacific coast of Oregon. The trip was expanding and enjoyable.

After two years I left behind the gray skies and rainy weather that make Portland so beautifully green. I gave each close friend a farewell piece from my art collection. When I go back to visit them, I see and enjoy my art in their homes.

When I moved to Denver to attend seminary, I didn't unpack much. Initially, I planned to reside there for only a few months, but stayed eighteen months. I used a spare bedroom of my campus apartment to store my packed boxes and only displayed enough art to make my apartment homey. Once again, I opened a local bank account and once again, I got free checking as an introductory gift. The storage unit, the

CHOOSE TO MOVE

credit union account, and the safety deposit box still existed in Florida. Even then, I was reluctant to pull up roots entirely.

When I wasn't sure where to go after Denver, I stored all the boxes and furniture in a wonderful storage unit built under a hill. It stayed cool all summer and I didn't worry about my art getting moldy or cracked. When I decided to move to Texas, I again rented a U-Haul to move my belongings. A friend from Denver drove with me in the truck. I did not own a vehicle at that time. This time, too, I gave each of my friends a piece of my art as a going-away ceremony. My art collection has been planted in many towns through the years.

After each move, I unpack boxes and discard more and more belongings. Soon after, I then buy a few new things to replace them. These replacements will remind me of that town after I have moved on. In Portland, I bought my dishes, bright red and yellow ones. In Denver, I bought my first bronze art piece, a statue of a moose, reminiscent of Alaska. In Austin, I bought several pieces of David Marsh's brightly-painted furniture that will always remind me of happy adventures in Texas.

Today, late in the moving saga, my personal belongings consist of a made-for-the-Northwest-forest-green love seat, a collapsible chair from Costa Rica, two green wicker chairs to match the sofa, a cedar chest my mother gave me, a double-bed frame and mattress set, a free-standing floor-length mirror, two black ladder-back chairs owned for thirty years, two floor lamps, one spindle take-apart bookcase, one card table, thirty-seven flats of art, a carved wooden bird collection, an assortment of blown glass and ivory carvings, three Revere Ware pans, a non-stick frying pan, two glasses, five mugs collected on my travels, six plates, silverware, four sheets,

52

one towel, one washcloth (when guests come, I let them go shopping to pick the color of towel they want), a box of books, lots of baskets, dried flowers, and rugs. I use these latter items for color and decoration and can leave them behind in the next move if necessary.

I went back to retrieve those poor, abandoned belongings in Florida. Since the unit was not climate-controlled, the roaches feasted on my picture albums and mildew covered the spinning wheel. However, most of the things were rescued and united with my personal belongings in Texas.

How much stuff do I need? I do mean stuff, as none of it has much market value, only memory value. I don't need a lot of furniture. I do need and collect original art and all things bright and colorful. These art objects remind me of happy times, of shopping with friends, of adventures with my son, or of my own unique being. They are all I really need.

Leaving My Friends

Leaving friends has been different than I thought it would be. I expected to lose my friends when I moved and to never see them again. Surprise! Many friends have stayed in touch and have come to visit—more than I ever would have imagined. I had visitors in Denver and Austin. I also went back for visits to Anchorage, Portland, and Florida. I make the effort to maintain friendships by writing about each new location and calling friends from time to time. I often get "Wow, we love getting your travelogues!" from those remaining behind who read my narratives.

In Anchorage, I found welcoming and helpful people. I had acquaintances who taught me how to make salmonberry jelly

CHOOSE TO MOVE

and took me hiking in bear country. In Portland, however, it was hard for me to make friends. I did a lot of Saturday road trips alone. Finally, I formed two close friendships including my present mentor. It took six months to feel like I belonged, and once I did, the leaving was very hard.

In San Diego, there were so many people but I never felt close to any of them. In Denver, my friends were fellow students in seminary. We debated social issues, borrowed eggs, and ate Saturday lunch together. When a blizzard hit, we all huddled together in campus housing and watched tree limbs snap under the weight of falling snow. Upper classmen and professors provided a supportive and safe academic cocoon. My friends from Portland and San Diego were coming to visit me as well. I began to realize moves don't necessarily mean I will lose all my friends—some really will stay in my life despite the physical distance between us.

One of the most important choices I made which helped me stay in touch with my friends was to have a long-distance telephone service with cheap interstate calling rates. I call my friends—my support web—a lot! In the early days of a move, when I am in a new neighborhood and city, I don't have friends to affirm me or listen to my story. So, the long-distance ones are a real blessing. I call often to share my dilemmas or my delight in a new adventure.

Today I have a group of friends who live all over the country. I have left them all, at one time or another. And yet, they are still in my life. Through them I share a larger world—weather, their politics, their daily lives. My life is also supported by their interest and encouragement. My friends are definitely one of the best blessings I have received from my moving adventures.

54

Leaving My Family

My moving from one city to another would have shocked my parents if they were alive, especially since I was motivated only by a desire to experience life in another city. In contrast, my brother and my son need no convincing. They support me in my decisions to relocate. My son loves to suggest more remote places than I have the courage to try, like a Polynesian island or Yellowknife in northern Canada. My brother still sends e-mails of his impressions of places he has visited for me to consider. Both have helped me empty an apartment, pack a moving truck, unpack it at the other end, and carry my belongings into a new home. My son has visited me in Portland, Denver, San Diego, and Austin even though he was living in Anchorage or Australia. Their emotional and physical support has helped me change places successfully.

Bread

I stand again before a strange bread shelf
Whispering ... it's ok, it's ok,
Holding back the tears.
Bread! You'd think so common a thing
Would be the same in everyplace.
Why is this moving so hard?
Why is even the bread, lowly goddamned bread, so strange?

I call up something from deep inside me
Something strong and brave
And reach out to the loaves
Looking for a new friend.
- First days in Denver

IN SUMMARY

With this information, I hope you have seen the ways that you can leave successfully. Leaving successfully is part of moving successfully. It involves creating the right circumstances and having the right attitudes. Leaving is hard work and necessary in order to make room in your life for the fabulous adventure you are about to encounter. This chapter ends the moving saga in the original community. Starting with the next chapter, we are in the new community and ready to make decisions that will assure a successful adjustment!

OTHER QUESTIONS TO THINK ABOUT

1. *What is your most valued possession?*

2. *Name five possessions you could not leave behind if you moved.*

3. *Name five possessions you could easily replace once you have moved.*

4. *Think of a time when you packed up your belongings—to go to college, after graduation, when you got married, when you moved to a new town—and recall the feelings you had then. Sadness? Anticipation? Nervousness? Uncertainty?*

5. *Remember when you unpacked your belongings. Did you feel excited? Surprised? Sad? Overwhelmed? What were your feelings at that time?*

Part Two
CREATING THE RIGHT LIVING CONDITIONS

3

Housing in Your New Community

CONSIDER THIS ...

Congratulations! You have successfully arrived in the place you have chosen for home. This can be a very exciting time. Your surroundings are new and a routine has yet to be created. And just when you thought you had the last decision behind you, now you have to decide about housing. This includes where you want to live and in what type of community.

Choosing a New Home

A wise housing choice can make the difference between a successful relocation experience and an unhappy one. Having an attractive, convenient, and safe living space can be important to your sense of contentment. It also can speed up the process of feeling that this is truly home.

You have many housing options. To help you sort through them, we will explore various housing choices as well as help you focus on your individual needs and lifestyle. In the *How I Did It* section, I will tell you how I chose my residences in such places as Austin, Anchorage, Portland, and San Antonio.

There are four aspects to consider. First, be aware of your lifestyle needs, perhaps by consulting your *Life's Essentials* list; second, be adventurous when choosing where to live; third, remember you can choose one situation for the short term and another for the long term; and finally, know that frustrations are normal.

A Home is More Than Shelter

For most people, a place to live is more than a shelter from the elements. A home can be a reflection of your personal interests and activities. Do you have a wonderful collection of Japanese bowls you want to display in your home? I collect Alaskan Native paintings so my living spaces must have broad expanses of wall.

A home can also be a refuge. Do you enjoy curling up with a book to escape the rush of the outside world? Choosing an apartment overlooking a garden setting may be wise if you want a tranquil setting. Your home may be the meeting place for friends. Will you want to have a group of friends over to watch movies or play cards? Will your home have room for these activities? Will you need your own space for privacy and relaxation, or can you share with a roommate? Your lifestyle needs should influence the decision you make for a living space.

Be Adventurous in Your Choice

Too often we put limits on our housing choices. I encourage you to consider all your options and explore exciting alternatives. The usual choices are between renting and buying an apartment, condominium, or house. These arrangements don't have to be in ordinary settings; you can choose an exciting place to live. For example, do you like to play golf or go to the gym? Why not live with a view of a golf course or within walking distance of a workout center? Perhaps you could find a place in the country that requires a few more minutes driving time but has broad vistas, big trees, and deer roaming across your lawn at dawn. Is there some famous landmark or outstanding feature located in your new community, like a vintage ship anchored in the harbor or a sandy beach? Why not live with a view of it? The residence and location you choose can create an extraordinary living experience.

In Denver, my campus-housing apartment faced west with the most glorious view of the Rocky Mountains that money could buy, and here I was, a student paying lowly student rent!

For the truly adventurous, there are even more choices. Alternative living choices may include living with friends who have lots of extra room, renovating an historical house, owning and living in a travel trailer, living aboard a boat, or caretaking a property. These choices can put whole new worlds at your doorstep. Be adventurous when you choose your housing!

You Can Choose Again

The third idea to remember is that you can make multiple housing choices, one for a shorter time and another for longer. As I describe in the *How I Did It* section of this

CHOOSE TO MOVE

chapter, I usually stay with friends or family in the beginning of a move. This gives me time to drive through neighborhoods and experience traffic flows, as well as time to recover from the stress of the move itself. Sometimes postponing a decision about an apartment or house can be a wise choice. In most cases, you will have time to wait.

Other choices exist for temporary housing beyond friends and family. A new kind of temporary housing has appeared in many towns. It offers suites of rooms for a short or extended period of time. Called executive suites, they meet the need of business executives who travel or need temporary housing. Staying here could be a comfortable choice if friends or family are not available for short-term stays.

Another plan for temporary housing is to rent an apartment for the minimum amount of time, usually three or six months, and move again once you are oriented in your new community. I am not a huge fan of this last option, because an unsatisfactory place can become familiar and it may be easier to stay even though it doesn't meet your lifestyle needs.

Choosing the best housing is an important decision that can take some time. It may be best to make a short-term decision and then choose again when you have more information, time, and energy to make that important long-term decision.

Feeling Frustrated Can Be Normal

Whatever you choose for housing, the decision-making process can be a frustrating one. It is driven by that sense of homelessness we have discussed. Most of us need a place to call home. Until we have that place, we cannot really feel settled, or even safe. There is urgency to the process of finding satisfactory housing. Try not to let that urgency take control. Keep

62

HOUSING IN YOUR NEW COMMUNITY

the frustrations to a minimum by knowing what your lifestyle requires, considering extraordinary settings, and by allowing yourself enough time to find the right and perfect home.

WEATHER

Weather conditions in your new home may be different. The climate may be colder or hotter than you are used to. Rain may rule for nine months of the year. The air could be thinner, drier, or breath-inhibiting humid. Hurricanes, tornadoes, and floods may visit this new place. In the course of moving, I have experienced a winter blizzard, a mild earthquake, and two spring floods. I moved from Florida to Texas and expected it to be a little colder in the winters and a little hotter in the summers.

> **I Dare You**
>
> *Greetings, Night!*
> *Not just sprinkling snow tonight*
> *You are heaving it at my doorstep.*
> *Cold, sparkling stuff this is*
> *And I am ready.*
> *My door is shut.*
> *I will watch your mischievous act*
> *From behind my blinded window.*
> *I sleep now.*
> *See how high you can pile it before I wake*
> *And peer again.*
> *-Denver*

Well, I was quite surprised and uncomfortable when the temperature got over 100 degrees for days on end, something that doesn't happen in Florida! Climate and weather changes will definitely affect your choice of a new home.

SPECIFICS OF HOME SELECTION

Finding your right and perfect home involves considering numerous specific aspects: housing budget, whether to rent or

CHOOSE TO MOVE

buy, length of stay, location, safety, community, scenery, living space, and furnishings. Now, let's discuss each of these areas.

The Housing Budget

Let's be realistic. The price of housing and what you can afford will be the major determining factor for what housing situation you actually choose. If you decide to buy, the price will determine the type of building you choose as well as its neighborhood and features. Considering condominiums rather than freestanding houses will probably be because of price. Whether you have a large backyard with a swimming pool, or no yard at all, will be influenced by price. Likewise, your selection of an apartment, house, or condominium to rent will be determined by what you feel you can afford. Make a budget. Know how much you have to spend before you go home hunting. Some choices may not be available to you because of price. Being adventurous does not mean taking on a bigger housing payment than is practical.

Rent or Buy

A fundamental decision about housing is whether to rent or own your living space. Each choice offers rewards as well as drawbacks. In weighing each alternative, look at the total cost of ownership of each choice. These include not only money, but also time, energy, and commitment. For example, the costs of buying can include down-payment money as well as time and effort to make repairs or modifications to the structure or yard. Costs of renting include rent money that will not grow as equity, the stress of knowing this is a temporary situation, and having transient neighbors. Your own cost lists may be different from these, but it is important to determine what your

HOUSING IN YOUR NEW COMMUNITY

costs for owning your own home is versus the cost of renting. Then decide which of these costs you can afford.

The choice to rent or buy will be influenced by three very practical aspects: your planned length of stay, the housing market, and your financial situation. Let's talk about length of stay first. If this move is a permanent one, then buying your own place is definitely a wise choice to consider. There may be tax advantages, equity buildup possibilities, and the opportunity to establish yourself in a neighborhood of other owners. Buying may also overcome the temporary stigma of being the newcomer. However, if you aren't sure how long you will stay or if you plan to stay less than two years, then consider renting. This way, you are free to move when you get ready and you won't have a house to sell.

Housing prices in your new community will also influence your decision to buy or rent. If the housing market is healthy, and housing prices are increasing faster than inflation, then buying a residence could be a profitable decision. Building equity for the future is an excellent thing to plan.

And finally, your financial situation will determine whether you buy or rent. If you purchase a home, you need enough cash for a down payment. This amount may be from five to twenty percent of the purchase price. Other expenses will have to be paid as well, like insurance and title fees. Don't forget the ongoing mortgage payments. On the other hand, if you rent you will have only the initial security deposit and the monthly rental fee to pay and an easy exit at the end of the leasing period.

Real estate agents, relocation services, and apartment-finding services can help you find suitable living arrangements. Many

65

CHOOSE TO MOVE

of them have homepages on the Internet you can use before you actually arrive. The Internet also carries many classified ads from metropolitan newspapers. These will give you an accurate idea of the housing market, including availability and price ranges, in the area where you are moving. The secret to success when you work with these professionals is knowing what you want. The more clearly you define your needs for your living space, the more easily they can help you find it.

Length of Stay

How long do you plan to stay? Don't be surprised by this question. As you have learned about me by now, I don't consider a move to be permanent. I believe it takes a long time to know if a community that's appealing for the first year will be suitable for many years. In the meantime, your stay will be temporary and your choice of housing will reflect that condition. The specific choices you make should best suit your needs for comfort, security, and economics. Depending on the length of your stay, your housing needs for space, furnishings, and ownership will be different.

First, let's consider a shorter stay, one of nine months or less. When I am a short-timer in a place, I want to spend my time outside exploring my new surroundings, not inside taking care of a large apartment. I don't usually bring furniture and I try to find a more inexpensive housing arrangement. Without furniture, I need less space to set up housekeeping. This is what I did in Denver when I attended seminary.

Furnishings also can be rented. This will add costs but will save the effort of moving and unloading these items. I haven't ever actually done this, but I have gone to see what is available. The furniture looked new and was stylish. As a furniture renter,

66

you are allowed to select the individual pieces that you want and you will be required to lease them for a definite period of time, usually six months or longer.

What about staying longer, for a year or more? Here are the criteria I use. If my stay is longer than a year in my new community, I usually bring my furniture with me. This way I have the comfort of having my own familiar belongings while I am settling into a new community. Furnishings will influence the size of the housing you choose. The more furniture you have, or the larger it is, the larger dwelling you will need. If you are considering calling this community your permanent home, think about buying your living space. Perhaps a condominium would be a better choice. You could live in it while you are in town and rent it out later if you decide to move. Do some research if you consider buying. Information about local growth can be found at the public library or from the local Chamber of Commerce.

Location

Another important consideration in choosing your home is location. Will it be convenient? How far is it to your workplace? How does the traffic flow in this location? These aspects can be easily overlooked in the haste to find a place because they are not as apparent as price or the decision to rent or buy. Yet these aspects are important.

The distances to businesses and services, as well as to the workplace, are also important. Frequented businesses may include a grocery store or health food store, a drug store, movie theater, or gym. Services such as libraries, post office, and schools are also important to consider. I always prefer to live close to where I work in order to minimize the driving time to and from the office. Is this important to you? Distance to work also has to be weighed against access to major roads and shopping areas. Would you like to walk to the local library branch? Would you use a fitness center more if it were nearby? Being a short distance from the grocery store, gym, pet store, and other businesses may be as important to you as living near work, especially if you work from home or are retired. If you don't own a car, then being near a bus route will also be important.

The flow of traffic near your home should also be considered. Do you want to live near a major street that is clogged with traffic most of the day? Does the neighborhood you are considering have multiple outlets onto streets with flowing traffic patterns? These advantages appear harder and harder to find in our age of more vehicles and fewer roads to support them. Will you have easy access to other parts of town by being near a freeway? Will you have to use toll roads to get to recreational or business destinations?

If you don't have answers to some of these questions, then spend time in the neighborhood at various times of the day. Show up during the morning and evening rush hours. Visit during the weekend. Drive in and drive out. In other words, try to anticipate the convenience or inconvenience of living in this location. Experienced every day, small inconveniences such as traffic and street repairs could spoil an otherwise excellent neighborhood.

Safety

The safety of the neighborhood where you plan to live is also important. This includes freedom from break-ins as well as being safe when you are outdoors. You can check on the

HOUSING IN YOUR NEW COMMUNITY

incidence of crime in your prospective neighborhood with the police or by asking residents. Will you feel safe walking in the early evening? Break-ins usually occur in darkness. You should look for bright street lighting so that no sections of the street are dark. This may require a visit after dark to observe lighting conditions. Also check to see that yards and gardens are maintained and that no trash is allowed to pile up near homes. Make sure the houses are painted and repaired. This isn't an absolute guarantee of a safe neighborhood, but it is an indication that this could be a safe place to live. If you are considering living in an apartment complex, look to see if a residential neighborhood is nearby. They are often safe places for walking and biking.

The safety of my living area is very important to me because I usually move and live alone. I worry less about my possessions being stolen when I make sure the outside area feels safe. I make several trips to the prospective neighborhood just to check on daytime and evening activity, lighting, and noise since I like to walk near my home rather than drive to a walking path.

Community

Community is best when your neighbors are like-minded and friendly and there is access to fun and enjoyable activities. Determining if your prospective neighborhood will be an enjoyable community is not easy to do. You can check for a swimming pool or workout room at a rental complex—that part is easy. But how do you know if the people who live next door are friendly? Are there other pet owners like yourself or will your neighbors hate pets? Will children and their noise disturb you? Do teenagers race cars or motorcycles down

69

CHOOSE TO MOVE

your street? Are bins for recycling glass and other materials available? Again, some of these things are easy to identify. Others cannot be known until you move in. Certainly you will want to drive through the neighborhood and observe. You might even stop someone who looks to be a resident of the area and inquire, "Do you like living in this neighborhood?" Ask specifically about roaming dogs, noise, or safety. It is your future. Don't be shy!

Scenery

What will be your view in this neighborhood? Do green spaces with trees and flowering shrubs exist? Will you have a panoramic view of the city lights? Every day you will come and go from your neighborhood and its scenery will be what greets you each time. For most of us, green spaces are renewing. So are the sights and smells of the ocean. Selecting a nourishing home means selecting a place to live with aspects of nature that are pleasing to your senses.

Living Space

Living spaces are as important as neighborhoods. Do you like new rooms with shine or older ones with character? Do you want to have a private outdoor area to relax in, like a deck or patio? Perhaps growing an herb garden or having a backyard for the dog is important. Do you want access to a pool or gym room? Do you want a view from the master bedroom? Do you want the morning sun shining in your bedroom or in your living room? If you are considering an apartment or condo, do you want to live on the top floor, with no overhead noises, or on the bottom floor with no stairs? What other things are important to you in the space where you live? Remember, you

HOUSING IN YOUR NEW COMMUNITY

can decorate over many things, but you cannot change the floor plan. Because this residence will be your home for at least the next few months, make the living space work for you.

Did you bring your surfboard or boat? Will that motorcycle need a place of its own? Do you want the ironing board set up all the time? Will you have regular visitors? Think about the amount of space you will need. This space is not just sheer volume to house your belongings, but space required for your comfort and convenience. Will an efficiency apartment or a one-bedroom apartment provide enough living space or will you need more rooms, perhaps for overnight visitors or for a home office? Do you like to spread out? Do you need extra floor space to exercise or dance?

If you are accustomed to living in a larger residence and move to a smaller home, the adjustment to having fewer closets and kitchen cabinets and less floor space may feel confining. Usually this feeling will disappear after a few months when your attention is directed to outside activities. Decorating with your favorite colors, art, and fresh flowers will also take your attention away from the smaller space and will make this place feel more like home. I can honestly say that I have never quite adjusted to living in a smaller apartment, but often I do it to save money.

Furnishings

Furnishings will influence your home choice. Is your furniture the Queen Anne style, tall and massive? Do you still own that sofa sectional or the triple dresser? If you have brought it this far, you probably want to have it in your home. It may even motivate you to select a more expensive housing arrangement. Another choice is to select more practical furniture. For example, when I began to move I traded my full-length sofa

71

CHOOSE TO MOVE

for a love seat and replaced my queen-size bed with a full-size. By doing this, I reduced the bulk of my furnishings as well as the hassle of moving them.

If you move without furniture, you will still need to have some basic pieces. At least three solutions exist for temporary furnishings. One is to rent a furnished living space. This may be an easy solution in the short term while you are still deciding how long to stay in this place, or whether to buy a place of your own. Another solution is to rent furniture separately. And the obvious solution to not having furniture is to buy some suitable pieces. Maybe all you need to survive for the moment is a kitchen table and two chairs. It's easy to add some bright placemats and a vase of fresh daisies to make a pleasant area. Think of this time as an adventure, one where you discover just how little you need to live comfortably. You will be in a position to furnish your living space exactly as you would like it, designer linens and all! Although I prefer having my own furnishings, I often leave my furniture behind and live with very little. I did that in Alaska where I bought a folding card table and lawn chair, and then added to them from garage sales and donations from departing friends. The whole Alaskan relocation experience is described in this chapter's *How I Did It* section.

HOW I DID IT

I wrote the poem about the brush during a frustrating time of searching for the right place to call home. I needed to feel settled but still had to do the hard work of apartment hunting. Not all my moves were so frustrating. As you will learn, I have chosen places to live that run the gamut of housing choices. They were always comfortable as well as safe and convenient places to live. In each place I chose a housing arrangement that met my esthetic, practical, and economic needs. Length of stay, size, location, and price were all aspects I considered seriously. As you will see, there are always trade-offs.

> ### The Brush
>
> *The brush ... where's the brush?*
> *Here somewhere*
> *Amid the boxes.*
> *I have dust and crumbs on my floor—*
> *I need my brush to clear them away.*
> *Oh God I want a home*
> *I want to belong somewhere and*
> *To have a shelf for my brush.*
> *It's ok It's ok*
> *I whisper and hold back the tears.*
> *Find the brush*
> *It's ok.*

AUSTIN

My first move away from my community of twenty-two years was to Austin, Texas. I was unsure of my ability to adjust, unfamiliar with the city, and uncertain the job would last. I did not bring furniture for this first move, which was a trade-off. I did, however, bring my cat and she and I lived with my brother for the first two months in Austin. This gave me a sense of security and a local source of information. Some days my presence put a strain on our sibling relationship. Eventually, we got reacquainted again as adults and became strong allies.

When I wanted my own space, I moved to an apartment in a nearby neighborhood. My cat was welcomed in the new apartment, too. My brother generously loaned me furniture.

CHOOSE TO MOVE

He moved it in, and later out, for me. The apartment I rented was far from work but near my brother, another trade-off. I was able to rent for three months at a time. This was fortunate because when the homesickness struck six months after moving in, I was able to return to my house in Florida without paying for an unexpired lease.

This first move was a learning experience for me, especially about housing. The housing choices available to me in Austin showed me that many options for housing are available in a new community.

GAINESVILLE

For the move to Gainesville, in north-central Florida, my housing arrangement looked brilliant on paper. I rented a room from parents of an acquaintance during the week and then returned to my Orlando home, two hours away, on the weekends. I had only a small income at the time and was waiting for a federal grant to fund my image-processing work at the university. Renting a room was an inexpensive solution. However, this solution did not turn out to be the happy choice it had seemed. The owners were an older couple and set in their ways. I suppose I was set in mine, too. Sharing a living room with strangers, having my bedroom cleaned over the weekend, storing my food on one small shelf in the refrigerator, and parking a block away did not give me the personal privacy and space I needed. The arrangement was just too close for all of us and I moved out near the end of my work assignment. For the last two weeks I stayed in a motel that was neither inexpensive nor homey but was a trade-off for privacy.

74

I considered price, safety, and location when I rented the room but it still wasn't a comfortable arrangement. Some plans just don't work out, regardless of how appropriate or practical they appear and how much analysis and visiting you do!

ANCHORAGE

My next move was to Anchorage, Alaska. In every way it was a grand adventure and I was ready! (I also must confess a secret advantage: my adult son moved there at the same time.) I loved Alaska for its ruggedness and beauty and intended to spend my salary on travel, not on a fancy apartment. From previous visits I had a few acquaintances. Moving furniture would have been costly so all I took was clothing and some favorite photographs. One of those acquaintances offered me her home for the first week and took me apartment hunting, where I soon discovered the choices were few. Therefore, I chose an unfurnished place in a bit of an unkempt neighborhood. Far from being fancy, my apartment was in a dimly-lit and heavily-trafficked neighborhood. I decided I would find other places to walk than along the major road that fronted my apartment building. Once again I made a trade-off, money for safety and scenery. Travel time was not a problem. With only 226,000 people in Anchorage, getting across town was a quick trip.

The apartment had one bedroom, a kitchen area, and a living area, plus a balcony that looked out to the Alaska Range. Furnishings included only the bare necessities, leaving big, open spaces. I filled them with green plants and bright rugs. I grew herbs on my second floor balcony and bought large baskets of red geraniums and blue petunias for my kitchen. I hung colorful posters by local artists on my walls and decorated

CHOOSE TO MOVE

with the few personal favorites I brought from Florida. Even though there were times when I missed having a soft bed and framed art on my walls, the sense of adventure about being able to do with so little was exhilarating. It was fun to be creative with my living quarters!

The front door of my apartment opened into an inside stairway I shared with another apartment. I was very careful to look ahead of me when arriving or leaving my apartment, not so much because I was afraid anyone would break in (I certainly didn't have any treasures to steal!) but more for my safety outside the apartment. When someone brought me home, often my son, they would wait to see me wave from the balcony before leaving.

Perhaps I was too nervous then, but I did what I needed to do to feel safe, short of paying a higher rent. Sometimes, part of an adventure is finding out how far beyond conventional safety you can go and still survive. I think that's what I was doing in Anchorage. And now that I have survived, it doesn't feel nearly as spooky a place as it felt then.

SAN DIEGO

By October, the reality of winter became apparent. By November, I was packing to move south and I arrived in San Diego before Thanksgiving. My dear friend Helen offered me a bedroom in her very large home and I moved in. This arrangement allowed us to take fun trips on weekends and share our busy lives on a daily basis. Her elderly mother lived with us and enjoyed having company in the house. My contribution was to research and suggest enjoyable places for us to take her mother on weekends. Once I found an appropriate park

HOUSING IN YOUR NEW COMMUNITY

or event, we'd bundle her up and off we went. She completely enjoyed these outings. Helen's sister, son, and daughter also lived nearby and I became part of a family. This was a new experience for me since death and divorce had dissolved my own family.

The house was very far from my workplace, another trade-off. Being the explorer I am, I would take a different way home from work or run errands on the way. The canyons would confuse my sense of direction and quite often I got lost—very frustrating to an explorer—and would arrive home later than planned, usually just in time for dinner. Helen's mother would hug me and say how relieved she was that I finally arrived. My feeble explanation was always, "I got lost again!" and she would reply, "Well, we are glad you are here now." It felt comforting to be cared for. The trade-off was doing without personal space in return for belonging to a caring family. I lived like this for two months.

PORTLAND

By this time I had been without my furniture for over a year. I really wanted to set up housekeeping with my own things. I wanted my own bed, framed art, and blue, seashell towels. So, when a lucrative job offer from Intel came, I moved to Portland and rented a two-bedroom apartment within a mile of my workplace. With my son's help, I rented a truck and transported my furnishings. I downsized my sofa and bed to make them easier to move. I brought my entire art collection, my new, smaller bed, my new, smaller sofa, assorted tables, a cedar chest to use as a living room coffee table, pots, pans, linens, and all my books. I felt as if I was making a real home for myself.

77

CHOOSE TO MOVE

Bringing my furnishings was a serious step because it meant I was becoming more invested in the new community. It also meant I was becoming comfortable on the West Coast when I had plans to return to Florida one day. Were those plans changing?

The apartment I chose was very comfortable and only a few years old. It was shaded by sixty-foot tall, majestic Douglas fir trees. They whistled when the wind blew and gave the area a rainforest smell. I put out birdseed that attracted finches, chickadees, jays, doves, and even an occasional gray squirrel. The neighborhood was safe and included quiet, residential homes nearby. Across the street was a farm with three cows, assorted geese, and one donkey. I felt comfortable walking in the evenings and often gave salutations to the cows.

I stayed in this apartment for almost two years. I explored the possibility of buying a condo but discovered property taxes were so high that I would have trouble covering my monthly expenses by renting it out. I still think buying is a wise option to consider when you plan to stay for over a year, but I made the right choice in this case.

A funny story about this apartment concerns those Douglas fir trees I liked. I arrived in January. By mid February, melted snows were causing flooding. Because the ground was saturated, tree roots could not hold and trees fell frequently. This was a phenomenon I had not experienced before. I worried about one falling on my apartment, especially after my apartment manager told me it could happen. I quickly bought renter's insurance and crossed my fingers. I'm happy to report no trees fell on my apartment while I was in Portland and I still think Douglas firs are wonderful.

DENVER

After Portland, I moved to Denver to attend graduate school. The college supplied apartments for those who wanted to live on campus. I moved into a second-floor, typical student apartment with an unobstructed westerly view of the Rocky Mountains. As students, we all agreed we would never again be able to afford such a fantastic, panoramic view. Sunsets were spectacular and my apartment had a front-row seat.

My classrooms were two hundred feet away and were a convenient walk during snow days. The campus was surrounded with stone and brick homes with manicured lawns. Parks with trails and ponds were nearby and walks in these neighborhoods were enjoyable. The school was on the main bus route and when I began to work downtown, riding the bus was very convenient. From my apartment on campus, I could even walk to the grocery store!

I moved from a two-bedroom apartment in Portland, where I had a spare room for storage, to a one-bedroom apartment in Denver. I had a dilemma: what to do with all my stuff, most of which I would not use while in school. For the first month, I rented a storage unit and put the excess belongings in it. But I really missed those furnishings and wanted everything with me. I am very attached to my possessions, though they are minimal! Laughing at myself, I rescued my possessions from storage, moved my bed into the living room, and converted the small, dark bedroom into a storage room for boxes, books, and the ironing board. I arranged the living area like an efficiency apartment, with a screen in front of the bed and the visiting area nearer the front door.

CHOOSE TO MOVE

Everything about the interior of the apartment was old. The wall surfaces were rough, the paint was dull, and the window screens didn't fit tightly. It had no dishwasher and the refrigerator was in the living room. But, it was cheap to rent. After awhile, this old apartment became comfortable like a worn slipper. I decorated with bright red and gold pictures of Native American women on horses, and put out fat cranberry, forest green, and white candles. My apartment was inviting, not stark like a traditional student's room.

That November, a blizzard dropped twenty inches of snow in two days. I had never lived through a real winter and having fellow students next door was reassuring. The blizzard inspired this poem.

> **Untitled**
>
> *Hushed ... warm ... inside.*
> *Snow ... cold ... sparkling ... outside.*
>
> *Total peace*
> *Inside my apartment womb*
> *For another spring snowstorm.*
> *I am home.*

SAN ANTONIO

When Denver, school, and a job all lost their appeal, I thought again about being near my family. I decided to move to San Antonio to be near, but not in the same town as, my brother. Finding a home in San Antonio was easy because my masseuse in Denver knew someone who had just bought a furnished house there and was interested in renting it for a few months. That was just the length of time I needed to adjust to San Antonio and find a place of my own. It was to be a vacation house for the owners and it was completely furnished, including silverware and linens. I moved all my furnishings and boxes into the garage.

The neighbors were friendly and mostly retired. I met gardeners and dog walkers. It was the first time I had lived in a house in a residential neighborhood since I left Florida. I had instant friends with whom I exchanged house visits and ran errands during the day since I was telecommuting from home.

After living in a residential neighborhood again, my tolerance for apartment living diminished substantially!

AUSTIN

I moved back to Austin, where there were more jobs and my brother lived. I rented an apartment that overlooked the skyline of Austin. On the Fourth of July, I had a ringside seat for brilliant fireworks!

IN SUMMARY

Each housing choice had its advantages and drawbacks. The apartment in Anchorage was not in a safe area, but it was cheap. The apartment in Portland was under gorgeous trees that could fall during the rainy season! The apartment in Denver was convenient but old. The house in San Antonio was roomy but not convenient to a bus line. Living with a family failed miserably in Gainesville but was an immense joy in San Diego.

Despite being a challenge initially, each place I have described became a pleasant, comfortable residence for me. I put down roots and made a commitment to be happy. I nested, decorated, and rearranged to make each place feel like home.

CHOOSE TO MOVE

The same choices will be available for you. Every housing option available to you will have pluses and minuses. Remember, where you live is more than a practical need for shelter. It is a refueling station, a meeting place for friends, a refuge from stress, and a reflection of the unique person you are. I encourage you to be creative with your living choices and to invest what you must in order to be comfortable, safe, and integrated wherever you live.

OTHER QUESTIONS TO THINK ABOUT

1. *Are you more comfortable with making arrangements ahead of time or with making arrangements after you have arrived and checked out the place? For example, will you need to have an apartment ready when you arrive or could you stay in a hotel for awhile and shop around?*

2. *If you were to move, how large an apartment or house would you like to have? What rooms would you like to have?*

3. *Would you enjoy having a yard with your home or apartment?*

4. *How far from work would you like to live?*

5. *What qualities would you require in a prospective neighborhood? Some suggestions are: safety, friendly neighbors, maintained yards, sidewalks, streetlights, children, light traffic, quiet, rural, urban, historic, or scenic.*

4

New Town, New Job

CONSIDER THIS …

Having a new job and relocating are inextricably tied together for most movers. Most of us need the income from a job to have a successful move. But a job can supply more than money. It can also provide intrinsic benefits like status and a social group. Your job can be a positive outcome of your move.

Likewise, moving can be a positive contributor to your work situation. Moving may benefit your career by providing more stimulating work. Sometimes the move will result in greater opportunities for advancement in your career.

In today's workplace, changing jobs is more tolerated and accepted than ever before. It is understood that very few jobs are permanent and that job changes can broaden and enhance a person's job skills. For those reasons, many people are now changing jobs frequently and enjoying the benefits.

If migrating to a new town is appealing to you, don't let the job issue stop you. This section will take a look at the intrinsic rewards of a job, what work arrangements are available, and will offer points to ponder to help you pick the right job. It will also discuss the trade-offs of having a job before you move versus getting a job after you move. And that worst of all cases, being without a job, will sneak its way into this chapter. As throughout the book, I will then describe my personal and sometimes daring work experiences in the *How I Did It* section.

IDEAS TO PONDER WHEN JOB HUNTING

Even though there are volumes written about choosing the right job and building a successful career, I offer you other ideas that may not be in those books. These ideas may give you a new way to look at your possibilities and to choose the right job for you. You definitely want to be sure the pay, environment, and responsibilities of any job are right conditions for you. But other factors are equally important: a job is more than money; this job may lead to the next job; time away is as important as time working; provided benefits are important; you can be adventurous about where you work; and your job can be the end or a means to the end. Let's discuss these one at a time now.

A Job Is More Than Money

A job can do more for you than provide money. A job can provide status for you as you are redefining yourself in your new community. For example, if you work for the largest employer in the area, you will have a certain standing in the community regardless of your job function. Where you work can define your peer group and be your introduction into the community at large. In Hillsboro, a suburb of Portland,

Oregon, Intel was the most highly-regarded employer. Those who worked at Intel were regarded as a special group by the rest of the community.

Where you work may influence your housing decision. If you want to live close to your workplace to avoid long drives, like I do, then you will look for housing near your workplace. This housing location may bring you to new neighborhoods or to the downtown area. In Denver I worked downtown for the first time in my career. My centrally-located apartment was only a half an hour away on a major bus line. I experienced a different living environment being near the center of a large city like Denver than the one I normally choose in the suburbs.

Jobs can also provide social contacts. This may be useful when you are new in the community and have few friends. In your work environment you come in contact with people who can recommend banks and car mechanics. They may share local events and offer moral support. However, as we will see, peers at work probably won't be permanent friends. Their main function for your move is to help you make the adjustments in the beginning.

And finally, having a job can structure your time. The work schedule required by most jobs may impose a welcomed routine in an otherwise chaotic time in unfamiliar surroundings. You will be forced to get up and go through the day, when otherwise you may remain unorganized. For all these possible rewards, having a job after a new move will benefit you in more ways than just having an income.

This Job Will Lead to the Next Job

When considering a work assignment, look beyond the present moment. Don't just be focused on the present, however

CHOOSE TO MOVE

pressing it appears. Regard this job as a doorway to the next job. Be sure it will open doors you *want* to open, not just ones you *can* open. Select work that excites and positively challenges you. Are you growing skills and knowledge for the next job? Is this job creating your future opportunities and opening those favored doors? From personal experience, I can share that at times I have been shortsighted during my career. I have taken convenient jobs only to discover the next job was harder to find because I had placed myself in a dead-end alley for jobs.

Time Away Is as Important as Time Working

Another consideration is the amount of time you will want to have away from the job. If you are a permanent employee, this will be spelled out in the amount of paid vacation time you are offered. Remember, this is negotiable at hiring time. If you work as a contractor, you can choose to take time between contracts to vacation and travel. In either case, getting the time you want is important. After all, you have moved to experience a fuller life. That usually won't happen inside the walls of an office! Those of us with wanderlust know that seeing the new territory *is* a high priority and we have to provide time and energy to enjoy it.

Along with having days off, also consider having flexible working hours. This has come to be known as flextime, where usually the only requirement is that you be present during core business hours in order to interact with your peers.

Benefits Are Important

Remember to negotiate the benefits you need from a new job. The benefits that come with permanent employment are insurance, 401K contributions, paid vacations, and paid sick leave. Are these benefits important to you and will you get them from the job? If they are not provided either because of company policy or because of your work status within the company, then you must provide the benefits you need for yourself. When my job doesn't provide medical insurance, I carry a policy for catastrophic medical expenses. When I can't participate in a retirement plan or won't stay long enough to become vested, I maintain investments in an IRA account.

Be Adventurous about Where You Work

Seek ways to let the job expand your possibilities. One example is to be open to working in different job locations. Perhaps this is the time to try working downtown if you have always worked in a suburb. Perhaps you will try working in a high-rise office building, where before you worked in a strip mall. I encourage you to be open to new job locations or conditions. You may welcome the change!

I can remember turning down offers for work in downtown Denver thinking how dreadful all the traffic, the noise, and the loitering homeless would be. Then the job offer came that I couldn't resist and it was downtown! There I was, riding the bus with other workers, dodging people on busy sidewalks, having infinite choices for a quick lunch—and liking it.

The End or a Means to the End?

Much has been written about the purpose of work and its role in our lives. For some, work is the goal itself, providing opportunities for personal growth and contribution. For others, it provides the means, mainly money, for meeting personal goals. The role our jobs play in our lives is a personal choice for each of us. Knowing what that role is will help create

CHOOSE TO MOVE

realistic expectations for job success and personal happiness. Will your job in this new community meet your goals of growth and service, or will it provide a means to meet those goals through outside activities?

In my own journey, I spent years evaluating the personal rewards of the career path I had chosen. I realized this path was chosen for its high pay and easy access to jobs. It did not enrich me personally and it did not fulfill my personal goals. Today the jobs I take are a means to an end. They supply me with ample money to live my true life including relocating to wonderfully stimulating communities.

What is your true life? Will your job serve that life or will it be the means that enables you to create that life?

EMPLOYMENT OPPORTUNITIES

Today's workforce has many forms, some that encourage relocation. Workers are now being hired as contractors, as free agents, or as telecommuters. Moreover, jobs are being structured as short-term, project-focused assignments. This gives you the opportunity to change jobs more often as well as relocate. It has been estimated that in the year 2004, seventy-five percent of all software developers and other front-line technology workers were contractors. Opportunities to change jobs and social approval for frequent career changes have increased tremendously. If you are open to a work status other than permanent employee, you will increase your job opportunities when you move.

Working As a Contractor

Being a contract employee is one option available to you in today's workplace. More workers are contracting their services and taking short-term assignments. Professions like nursing, teaching, engineering, and construction all employ contract workers. A contract worker may work directly for a company as an independent contractor, or for a recruiting company who then places the W-2 contractor into a position at a company. This is in contrast to a permanent employee who gets paid directly by the organization they report to every day. Each work arrangement has its advantages and disadvantages. You will have to decide which suits your needs the best. This is a complex topic. Let me simply characterize each option.

The contract worker usually has a short-term horizon for an assignment, less than a year in most cases, and takes home more cash in each paycheck. They do not get paid vacations, paid sick leave, 401K opportunities, or salary bonuses. They don't earn a salary but are paid hourly. They are paid for every hour they work and they set their working hours in agreement with the company. They may or may not pay their own taxes and insurance. On the other hand, the permanent worker is included as a member of the company, gets benefits including paid vacation time, retirement plans, and pay raises, and usually takes home less money in their paycheck than the contract worker. Their equivalent hourly rate is less because they get these other benefits. They are usually required to put in the time to get a project completed, regardless of the pay involved.

Working as a Free Agent

Another work arrangement is to be a free agent. In this arrangement, a person works for himself or herself. Businesses hire free agents directly. Under this arrangement, free agents pay their own taxes and insurance. Some companies prefer this arrangement because they have lower overhead costs for the

CHOOSE TO MOVE

employee. Each state has defined this working relationship and most states require some sort of license, so do your research before taking this direction.

Telecommuting

An interesting development in some fields is telecommuting. Remember those predictions of a worker in their living room typing away on the computer while talking to the office four hundred miles away? Usually, a child, pet, or spouse was pictured to show the worker's connection with home life. Remember the hype that centralized workplaces would cease to exist? Well, we haven't come that far, but it is now electronically possible to work from your home and have a successful career, especially in the high-tech industry. The secret to finding a company willing to let you work this way is to start as an on-site employee and then gradually move into doing work from home. Perhaps only a portion of what you do daily can be done from home. Start there. Once you have this arrangement, you can include it on your resume and make it a condition of employment for the next company. How does this affect your moving destination choices? It may expand your choices of interesting places to live because you no longer are restricted to locations where you can get a job. Now you can move to a Caribbean island, a cabin in the Rocky Mountains, or live aboard a sailboat.

MAKING A CAREER CHANGE

Being willing to make changes in your career may also increase your job opportunities. Relocation presents a perfect time to try something new. When you are thinking of moving to a new place, you can also decide to change careers or try a different type of work. For example, a computer engineer can become a college professor in the new community. Then later, they can return to engineering. A developer of products can become a technical writer describing the use of those same products. A public librarian can try being a university librarian. Moving may provide opportunities to change the type of work you do. Stay open to those opportunities as you search for your job in the new place.

Do I Find a Job Before or After I Arrive?

Most moves are motivated by a change of jobs, so the job comes before the move. On the other hand, if you move like I do and consider the job a secondary importance to having the right location, then getting a job may be done after you arrive. In either case, each scenario has its trade-off.

If you want to have a job before you arrive in your new home, the Internet can be a big help. It has sites for jobs from newspapers in your new community as well as sites for posting resumes and available positions. Having a job before you arrive may assure that the money you need for moving and afterward will be available. This affords peace of mind for at least one aspect of the move. It may also help you choose a home location because you will know where your workplace is located. Once you are given an offer, gather as much information as you can to assure you are making a prudent choice. If you can visit first, do that.

If you move first and then start your job search, you may experience a few sleepless nights. As you get your resume in top form, begin to network within your community. As you find jobs that suit you, your confidence will grow. The obvious advantage of waiting until you move is that you will

CHOOSE TO MOVE

have more information to make a job choice. Employers are more favorable to applicants who live in the area and are putting down roots. Selecting where to live also has a benefit. If you have made temporary housing arrangements, like staying with friends for the first few weeks, then you can shop for a job and find convenient living locations at the same time.

What about qualifying for an apartment without a job? When my friend Irene relocated, she didn't have her next job yet. When she found the apartment she wanted, she told the manager her situation and was accepted based on her savings. So, remember to try many options.

BEING WITHOUT A JOB

Being jobless is one of life's more unpleasant, stressful circumstances. How are you going to deal with it? Here's a six-day routine you might try. On the first day, stop your job searching and play instead. Take a drive in the country, go swimming, go to an art museum, or do some activity you will really enjoy. Get outside if possible. For one day, forget about job hunting. At the end of the day, find a way to relax. I relax with candles and a warm bath. Get in touch with any feelings of fear and anger. Let these feelings exist. They may tell you about changes you need to make in your work life or in your outlook. Ask yourself, *What do I really want to be doing for work?* Give the answer a few days to find its way into your consciousness.

On the second day, do some strenuous exercise. Take a longer than usual walk, or give the treadmill a workout. After that, write down a plan for job hunting. Include in that plan a trip to the library or bookstore to read books about finding your right job. Also include surfing the Internet for a job. You are taking the first positive steps to getting the job you want. On

92

NEW TOWN, NEW JOB

this day, think of other scary times in your life. How did they turn out? Probably just fine, even though you were scared. On the third day, start your plan. Do some action that gets your search outside yourself. Make a call, mail a resume, or send an e-mail. The next day, do the same. Job hunt for four days, then take another day to play. For the next day, exercise and re-evaluate your plan and check off items you have completed. Notice the positive progress—things are getting done. Cross off or change other tasks on the list. Repeat this pattern of play day, exercise and plan day, then four job-hunting days for as long as it takes to find a suitable job.

Throughout this time, it is extremely important to have someone available to call who can see the big picture for you, the picture of your safety and prosperity. It is also important to eat healthy and watch your sugar and alcohol intake. Sleep your regular amount of hours, and set the alarm clock if you are tending to sleep longer than usual. Signs of depression include sleeping longer than normal as well as not being able to sleep.

During the writing of this book, I have taken time away from a job to concentrate on writing. It has been a scary thing for me to do. At the end of the allotted time, I had to get a job. Here, briefly, is how I weathered that most trying session of job hunting. I hope it will give you comfort and a smile.

First, I kept a mentor on call for the panic attacks. She agreed I could call day or night if the fears took control of my sanity. My mentor invited me to picture a scary time and how it turned out. I thought of how nervous I get when I go snorkeling where I can't touch the bottom. The reality is that I am safe, but I feel scared. I realized that feeling scared is not a sure sign

93

CHOOSE TO MOVE

that I am in danger. Likewise, being scared when I don't have an income is not a sure sign I will wind up a bag lady.

For my play day I drove to a beach where large, green sea turtles were just at the water's edge. For my exercise day, I went to a water aerobics class and pounded that water for all I was worth! Afterward, I went to a discount clothing store and bought black lace underwear! This was for self-confidence when I wrote those difficult cover letters! In a few days, my fear spoke to me about what my real talent was in the computer field. A few weeks later, I found my right and perfect job.

HOW I DID IT

I have always needed to work to have the money to relocate. Sometimes the availability of a job determined where I would move; other times, I wanted to move to a certain town and I found a job after I arrived. Two of my moves were the results of accepting lucrative jobs in interesting cities, one in Portland and the other in San Diego. These were some of the earliest moves I made. In later moves, finding a job was secondary to the location choice. I had acquired the skills and confidence to find work and I didn't have to depend on having a job first before I could move. The only requirement I made for a destination was that it be a larger town so I would have many opportunities for finding work.

Austin

When I moved to Austin, I had a job waiting for me because I started my job search before I left Florida. I found it by networking with a professional organization that had

NEW TOWN, NEW JOB

branches in Orlando as well as in Austin. The job itself was in a two-person office doing a little bit of everything. It was one of those jobs that was going to lead to something really unique and interesting or it was going to be a disaster. It turned out to be a disaster, and I chose again. It wasn't fun job-hunting for a second time in six months! This time I found a job by contacting Austin recruiting agencies. I was hired as a contractor in a large company doing the software programming I was used to doing.

The first job could have had many rewards and could have opened doors for a career change; the second had all the practical rewards of money, resume fodder, and learning new skills, but was not a career change. Although I did not stay in Austin for a long time, those work experiences began to give me the confidence that I could find employment and have an income wherever I chose to move.

GAINESVILLE

When I moved to Gainesville, my second attempt to relocate, I was working with the large state university located there. I went without pay because it was an opportunity to work in a new field in the public sector. I stayed on as long as I could financially. During this time I collected unemployment benefits and searched everywhere for jobs. It was a humiliating and stressful time in my career. Recession raged in our country and defense contracting was being cut drastically, so finding work was hard. I hoped working in the public sector in a new field would expand my skill set. Perhaps it would lead to satellite data-retrieval work, a field I thought would be challenging. However, I never got paid and never made a career change. This job resulted in receiving intrinsic rewards,

CHOOSE TO MOVE

like status, structure, and support, rather than money. Just as my savings for this adventure were running out, I got a job offer to enter the world of software testing, which turned out to be a career change for me. This job was in Orlando and I returned home.

ANCHORAGE

I managed to stay in Orlando for just over a year when the economy improved and wanderlust struck again. This time, the desire to move came before the job choice. When I decided to go live in Anchorage, I subscribed to the Sunday edition of the local newspaper and answered every employment ad appropriate for my experience. By the time I moved, I had three interviews waiting and one very lucrative job offer. I took the job offer as a permanent employee and went to work on an Air Force base for a private defense company. Every day I watched F16s do practice runs. Once, the Russian Air Force came for a friendly visit to exchange flight knowledge. (As far north as Alaska is, the enemy is more Mother Nature than another country!) It was a wonderful place to work. The money was ample, and I was involved in an interesting project to support Civil Defense rescue missions. My boss even brought in freshly smoked salmon when he went fishing!

When the contract ended with the Air Force, we moved back into an office building in downtown Anchorage but had no work to speak of. It was November and cold weather, darkness, and snow set in. I felt a need to go south, being the Florida-bred person I was. I began to review jobs available at the San Diego branch of this company and found an appropriate opening.

96

SAN DIEGO

I was transferred to San Diego to work on a new project to track secret documents for the military. In this move, the job preceded the destination; that is, I moved to San Diego because of the job. I was not really interested in San Diego but friends had suggested it might suit me. (Would you believe at this point I was still looking for a place to settle and had no idea the relocations would continue for several more years?) I found that I neither liked the job nor the city with all its cars and wall-to-wall people. I was used to a slower pace and less of everything. I suppose having been in Anchorage where stores are accessible and people are helpful had spoiled me for a large California city. I began to send out resumes again, but only to select cities on the West Coast and only for contract positions of short duration.

PORTLAND

A few months later I got a call offering me a job in Portland for twice the money I was currently earning. I immediately accepted it never having been to Oregon in my life! This was a tremendous advancement for my career as well because the job offer was from Intel, then the leading computer-chip manufacturer. I remember with a smile the conversation I had with the recruiter. When he told me the job was with Intel, I stopped him and said, "I think you have misread my resume. I only test software, not hardware. I'm not sure, but doesn't Intel do something with hardware?" At the time, I didn't even know who Intel was other than knowing they made something for computers. He assured me Intel also produced software, although not as publicly as they produced hardware. This story

CHOOSE TO MOVE

ought to be a reminder that some jobs, the ones we are really meant to have, just seem to find us despite our ignorance!

I stayed with Intel longer than the original six-month contract, longer than the next one-year contract, and longer than the last three-month contract. In all, I worked twenty-three months and acquired some fantastic job skills. My resume was glowing after this assignment. This job offered me the extrinsic reward of a high salary as well as the intrinsic rewards of status, a support system, and life in an interesting, agricultural suburb. From the experience of working at this leading company, I learned valuable skills that advanced me in my career for the next ten years. However, this was my first exposure to the stresses of a large corporate setting and I succumbed to burnout. After almost two years, I needed a change.

DENVER

Next I chose to accomplish a lifelong dream of attending a Methodist seminary. The best one for my purposes was in Denver, Colorado, so I packed my bags and moved. This was another attempt to move my career in a new direction. I wanted to become a corporate chaplain, dealing with the psychological and emotional problems workers in a high-tech environment encounter. Most students were studying to become pastors of local churches. I was the exception there. I learned how rapid change in the workplace affects the worker, how to minister to personal problems, and how to counsel for a career change. I learned to articulate the stresses in my own high-tech environment. I listened to stories of Native Americans, African-

New Town, New Job

Americans, and gays. After these experiences, I became a more enlightened citizen and a more compassionate caregiver.

After a year, I decided to go back to work and attend school part-time. The job market in Denver, as in the rest of the United States, was strong. At first I turned down offers to work in the city. I worried about the safety of being downtown alone. (Like one can be in a large city's center and be alone!) You will not believe the next part of this story. When I eventually did agree to an interview with a company located downtown, I had to have a friend meet me as I got off the rapid transit train because I was so afraid. It doesn't seem possible, does it? I actually cried on that ride and was afraid to stand on the street alone. I pretended to look at the store window displays until my friend arrived. She was all of twenty and thought I was crazy! My interview was with a small startup company in a high-rise office building. I remember asking the lobby attendant how many floors this building had and was shocked when she replied, "Thirty-two, honey." I didn't know a building in Denver could have thirty-two floors! I just did not know about cities back then.

I took the job and rode the bus and rapid transit every day from my campus apartment. I learned to enjoy the evangelists and itinerant musicians occupying the street corners, and ate many wonderful lunches downtown with my colleagues. I learned to enjoy working downtown and continued there for almost a year.

And then came the opportunity to telecommute. You won't believe this part of the story either. I announced to my company that, true to my goal of not staying in Denver for a long time, I was leaving. I didn't really have a city in mind, but I

99

CHOOSE TO MOVE

was ready to leave Denver. Because of the contribution I had made, my company offered to let me work from home and return to the office periodically. They also offered to change my employee status from contractor to salaried employee. I accepted, thinking this would only last a few short months. Off I went, job in hand. I spent another summer in Portland with my friends at the Saturday farmers' market. After three months of telecommuting from Portland, I moved to San Antonio, and worked remotely for another five months. My computer desktop was littered with icons for Internet connections to each city—Denver, Portland, San Antonio, and Austin. It was an unsettled time for me. I thought I should be settled down by now.

Finally, the time came when the company and I mutually agreed to end my telecommuting position and my connection to Denver.

AUSTIN

After San Antonio, I moved back to nearby Austin for a year and took a job in the downtown area. Working downtown was as much fun as it had been in Denver and with fewer traffic hassles. The bus ride downtown became a highlight of my day, although I still had offers of rides from friends who did not understand my love of bus riding and the opportunity it afforded to unwind. The lunchtime choices included Mexican, Thai, and Greek. Once a month we'd take a ten-minute walk to the cafeteria in the Texas State Capitol and eat in the company of lawmakers.

Because of positive experiences working downtown, I am partial to that location if I have the choice.

100

As I conclude writing this chapter, I am considering going to work in Australia because that's where my son lives. I will have to find a company who will sponsor me, at some considerable cost to them. Or maybe I will work in Hawaii and experience island life and that ever-perfect climate.

Next time, the location will precede the job. And whatever the location, I will make the contacts I need to find a job and move successfully.

IN SUMMARY

Whether the move or the job comes first, a successful job search requires consideration of many factors, as we have seen. Most of all, it requires confidence and perseverance. Do not let having a job diminish your choices for a move or stop you from moving. Have courage, have patience, and have faith. Opportunities for jobs are everywhere and some job will be right for you. Set your goal on the move and the job will follow!

CHOOSE TO MOVE

OTHER QUESTIONS TO THINK ABOUT

1. *Would you be willing to take a "survival" job if you couldn't find a job in your field of experience?*

2. *Name three ways you would find a job in a new town.*

3. *Will you need the income from a job when you move?*

4. *How long could you be without an income after moving?*

5. *How employable are you?*

6. *Is the information on your resume current?*

5

Making Friends

CONSIDER THIS ...

We go through a certain evolutionary process of acquaintanceship, friendliness, and friendship. The last implies a commitment to the relationship. Everyone knows very well the experience where we relate to an acquaintance whom we cultivate and get to know and gradually reach a place of commitment to him or her. Commitment is what characterizes friendship. We can walk away from casual acquaintances, but we cannot walk away from friendship once it has been established without breaking somebody's heart, including our own.
– Thomas Keating, in his book Intimacy with God

I believe we all need friends in our lives, people with whom we can share and have fun. Part of the process of becoming rooted again in a new community is finding people who share your interests and values and who have the potential to become supportive friends. Abraham Maslow has said, "You cannot grow without community ... [and] society." I would add that

CHOOSE TO MOVE

you cannot have a successful moving experience without a community of friends.

Having the right attitude is essential to making and keeping close friends. Thomas Keating, in the opening quote, said that commitment was an essential ingredient of friendship. I would add patience and a sense of adventure to the list of right attitudes for making and keeping friends.

In this chapter we'll examine how these attitudes can produce results and make your move a success. Dating, web friends, and a new concept I call *first friends* will also be discussed. As always, this chapter will include my own experiences of making friends and creating a family for myself. They are numerous and creative!

SUGGESTIONS FOR FINDING FRIENDS

Your first few months in a new place may be the only time in your life that you will welcome a red blinking light on your answering machine, and the only time when you won't see it because it is hidden behind an unpacked box. You will want friends when none seem to be available. Feeling the need for friends at this time is a normal reaction to leaving familiar friends and routines behind. The truth is, it takes time to connect with people in a meaningful way. For example, it takes a few conversations to learn that you both live on the same side of town, or to explore common interests and shared values. I don't know the magic or the day, but I do know the connection to friends will happen.

Have Guidelines

Do you look for certain traits or qualities in potential friends or do you just let friendships happen? Being clear about what

I want from a friendship helps me make friends faster and ensures the friendship lasts longer. Here are the questions I ask myself:

First, do I enjoy being with this person? Do we share common interests or activities? These shared elements provide a bond over time.

Second, does this person live a balanced life—eat healthy, stay rested, have a positive outlook? I have discovered that a person cannot treat me nicer than they treat themselves. And a happy, healthy person is just more fun to be with.

Finally, will this person meet me halfway? I want a friend who will take turns initiating activities, one who will expand my universe with their own experiences and suggestions as well as be open to mine. This is how I like to grow in friendship.

Think about your own desires for friendship. Having guidelines for a potential friend will help you recognize them when they appear in your life.

Common Interests

The best way to meet people who might become friends is to engage in activities you like and enjoy. This puts you in the company of others who share these interests. Common interests are the one best thread for weaving a friendship. It is these common interests that sustain friendships over time and build a history of shared experiences. Listen for interests you have in common, like sports, movies, or art. Ask the person to do something with you, or just call them and chat. It may take several tries and left phone messages before you each find the time to visit.

Pay attention if the other person doesn't respond to your calls or invitations. Perhaps they don't have the time for a friendship or their social needs are met. Give them a blessing and move on. Friendships have a life of their own, nourished by the interests and needs of each of you. It is like a dance. One takes a step; the other takes a step. It is not a dance if only one set of feet is moving.

One way to find out what is important to someone is to notice what is on the front of their refrigerator door. This is the place most people put favorite pictures, sayings, and reminders. Mine currently has my latest underwater fish photographs and sayings about abundance.

Organizations

Attending meetings of groups that share your interests is another clever way to meet people. If you belong to national organizations, you can maintain that association by finding a local chapter nearby. Most of the environmental organizations, like Audubon Society, Native Plant Society, and Sierra Club have chapters and meetings all over the United States. The same is true with social organizations like University Women, Rotary, and League of Women Voters. In addition, there will be local organizations that only exist in your new community. These may include sports, music, and environmental groups. Denver has an active skiing club, Austin has the Medieval Music Society, and Portland has an organization that teaches and builds straw-bale housing. Others may include film societies, recycle groups, and opera guilds. Check them out. Then get out and participate. You can't make friends sitting home alone.

Your Day Job

Another avenue to meet appropriate people for friendships is through your work, or your school if you are a student.

At work you both share a common interest in the company that employs you. You may also share a common schedule or project. Everyone goes out for lunch, everyone takes mid-afternoon snack breaks, and everyone celebrates TGIF after work on Fridays. Not literally everyone, but you get the picture. Working or attending school offers opportunities to more easily find out about your colleagues or fellow students.

But beware of a possible drawback. Sometimes friendships through work can be disruptive if they are dissolved with bad feelings. You may have to see or interact with your ex-friend at work. To sum this suggestion up, friendships through work may be easier to start, easier to maintain, but difficult to live with if they end before the job does.

Attend Church

Attending church can be a non-threatening way to meet people. Most churches will extend a warm welcome to new-comers. And rather than just attending the larger services where meeting individuals is harder, attend a smaller class or group for opportunities to get acquainted and to establish common interests. Many congregations serve coffee and other refreshments after the main church service, so plan to linger afterward. It may take several tries at different churches to find a comfortable community, but it can happen.

Take a Class

What interest do you have that you would like to learn more about or what do you know nothing about but wish you did? Classes abound for the skilled and the unskilled these days. These classes are fun choices for pursuing your interests. Whether you meet potential friends or not, you will at least

CHOOSE TO MOVE

have some new knowledge to enjoy. Almost every high school, university, or community college offers adult learning classes for personal enrichment.

Neighborhood recreation centers also offer classes for exercise, dancing, hobbies, sports, and nutrition. Art supply stores offer classes about art hobbies. Sports shops offer classes on fishing, first aid, and hunting. Hiking and bike stores offer classes on outdoor activities. Health food stores provide cooking classes. The list of sources for classes is endless and the subject areas for classes are wide-ranging.

I have taken classes in career planning, finding a mate, packing for a trip, living simply, bead making, fly fishing, apple preserving, sign language, and cat behavior. I enjoyed them all! The important question is: What do *you* want to learn about?

Volunteer

Volunteering can also serve as an avenue to find new friends. Whether you find a new friend or not, you will have given your time and energy to make the world a more peaceful place and that's significant. Volunteer opportunities are wide-ranging and include stuffing envelopes for the opera, being a museum docent or nature park guide, mentoring a child, working at Hospice, teaching someone to read, or providing pet care at the Humane Society. They all can be fulfilling ways to spend your early days in a new community!

You can also volunteer to help those you know—your neighbors, church acquaintances, or coworkers. They need help, too, and it will provide a chance to get more acquainted. For some specific ideas, read the *How I Did It* section that follows, where I share some ways I volunteered for those I knew.

TYPES OF FRIENDS

A friend can be someone you see on a regular basis, have fun with, and have known for years. A friend can also be a chat room pal, a date, or an early friend, the concept I call *first friend*. A very special friend can also become family. Each of these friendships has its rewards.

Across the Web

One kind of friend you may have is one you get to know through your computer. Yes, finding friends can be done electronically these days! There are many chat rooms and sites on the Internet where you can post your information and "meet" others of similar interests. They may even live in your town, or have information to share to help you get settled. Because these friendships are not restricted to your physical location, you can start the search before you leave your hometown. This can be one way you will not be dependent on that phone to ring or that red light on your answering machine to blink!

Dating

Then there's the whole dating aspect of friendships. If this is something you want in your life, stay open to these possibilities. These friendships can be very attainable in your new community. There are several ways to meet prospective dates. One way is to join a singles club and go, however hard it is, to the activities they offer. These may include dances, hikes, picnics, and skiing.

Another way to find dates is through the local newspaper. Most offer personal ad services and often sponsor events for singles. The ads are amusing to read, and are generally expensive to answer. Phone rates can be two dollars per minute.

Writing and placing your own ad is a productive way to get clear about what you want in a partnership and to put this out to the world. When I placed personal ads, they resulted in enjoyable conversations with interesting men and useful information. I learned about a Cajun dance club in Portland and about an antique district in Denver. Did I meet anyone I wanted to date? No. So, having realistic expectations is important. However, many people have found suitable partners just this way—you may get lucky, too.

The First Friend

Sometimes friends serve a limited purpose and only last a few months. Those who come early and do not last, I call *first friends*. These are the people who have an instinct for those of us who are new in town. They are the ones who know the directions where we need to go, can recommend doctors, dentists, and hairdressers, and who have unlimited time to share. These people are angels in their own way. They fill that initial time when you don't know anyone and want some kind of human companionship around.

However, because these types of friendships are not built on common interests, they usually do not endure. They are only for surface situations. These initial friendships fail for another reason. You aren't emotionally stable enough to show up and be committed just after a move. You are still trying to figure out who you will be. As you settle down, your interests and activities will change, and so will these early friendships. Enjoy them while they last.

I approach these friendships, which occur each time I move, with appreciation and awareness of their value for that time in my life. I usually value later friendships more than ones

MAKING FRIENDS

formed early after a move. Both play important roles in the success of a move.

Once you are settled, you can become *first friends* to the next newcomer. You can enjoy being someone's *first friend* by driving them around town, meeting them at the farmers' market, and introducing them to your friends.

Extended Family

On the other end of the continuum from *first friends* is a friendship that goes beyond the normal commitment of being friends. I refer to these as family relationships. These are relationships with people who celebrate your life and encourage your desires, regardless of whether they are people you grew up with or not. These are the people who will share the journey of your life, step by step and prayer by prayer. When you are in need, they show up. When you lose your focus, they echo it back.

Even more than friendships, these kinds of family relationships survive the passage of time and the interruptions of distance. It is a miracle I cannot explain. And sometimes, family just appears when you need it the most. There is no magic formula I can give you to make these saints appear, but I assure you they will appear.

My extended family has come in many forms. I am fortunate that my brother and my son always support my decisions to move. They are the part of my family that has existed from the beginning. Other family members have been cultivated out of friendships that already existed. My mentor, my friend since childhood, my moving miracle, Irene, and the seventy-two-year-old woman who taught me about reef fish are also part of my family.

111

Pets

A pet can be a very loyal friend during and after a move. Until you are settled into a new community, having a pet or adopting a new one may help you both. Pets are wonderful family substitutes and will love and be with you for your favorite activity as well as in the isolation of the night. Remember, this kind of friendship also requires commitment, so be prepared to give as well as to receive.

Solitude Solutions

Loneliness is a common side effect of changing places and it may be one of the unwanted parts of your move. Not only are you without the comforting familiarity of friends, family, and social events but you may also not know anyone when you move. Sometimes you may find yourself alone and needing to be around people, especially if you are a single mover. You may crave the sound of a familiar voice. One solution is to go to places where people are having fun, like bookstores, coffee houses, or parks and just hang out. You will feel connected just by being around others.

My favorite trick is to find the nearest bookstore with the softest chairs and spend a few hours reading and observing over the edge of my book. Or I may go to a park and walk with other exercisers. I find that just hearing other voices or seeing people having fun is enough to dispel my lonely feelings.

A friend of mine escapes solitude by walking the aisles of an all-night pharmacy. This may not be pretty but it works. Being around people will help, so find those opportunities. Usually, these lonely feelings will decrease as your social calendar begins to fill and you make friends in the new community.

MAKING FRIENDS

HOW I DID IT

Of all the gifts I have received from moving, the most valued are the friends I have made and the skills I have acquired to make friends easily. This skill was grown over many moves. It was hard at first until I developed the right attitudes for making friends. Now I know that making friends is mostly about showing up at activities and letting enough time pass for the meeting to develop into an ongoing friendship.

Today I have many wonderful friends who live in various cities and who get excited about my adventures. They send favorite foods, come to visit me, and support the life I have chosen. Many of them qualify for family status and for them all, I am too grateful for words.

AUSTIN

Making friends in Austin was difficult because this was my first attempt to move to a new town. I had lived in Orlando for almost twenty years and raised a family before I began moving. I had many friends. In Austin, things were very different. I had to make an effort to find friends who shared my interests.

I attended a class at the local university on how to pack for a trip (and learned that you don't need to take an outfit for every day you are traveling). But no friends resulted from it. I attended a Baptist church where I liked the preaching. During one of the mid-week dinner gatherings, I met the one friend I had in Austin. I learned we lived in the same neighborhood. From that we progressed to walking her dachshund in the evenings. She liked to shop and would take me along. She was the first person who ever tried to convince me I needed to own

113

CHOOSE TO MOVE

the latest fashions. When she succeeded, my wardrobe took on a new personality—like the time I bought a skirt that didn't cover my knees. Remember, I was over fifty by this time!

I also volunteered for Hospice training and met people with similar beliefs as mine. This would have been the beginning of making some friends. However, I did not stay long enough to grow these beginnings into meaningful friendships.

I even tried to date in Austin. I joined a singles club for the first time. Although it was fun perusing male members' profiles, the actual meeting experiences were not enjoyable. I was not sure of myself or what I wanted. I also learned to dance country-western style and felt like I was almost a true Texan. I was very shy in those days and usually just danced and went home. I didn't realize I had to make a conscious effort to meet people and take time to get to know them.

When I joined my brother in Austin, I discovered we had very different interests as adults. My expectation of his filling all my companionship needs was replaced by an understanding that we would not see much of each other. My solution was to develop a new definition of family that included those who cared for me and supported me. This began to heal the loss of family I experienced with my brother. And once I ceased expecting so much of him, we became committed friends.

These early attempts to find friends and create family were not very successful. But these experiences helped me grow the skills and attitudes necessary to find and keep friends.

ANCHORAGE

In contrast, making friends in Anchorage was easy and natural. Everyone accepted me—flannel shirt, jeans, and

MAKING FRIENDS

all—from day one and they were willing to form friendships quickly. Family ties, using my definition, endured because winters were cold and dark and you often depended on your neighbor to survive.

In the beginning, my son and I stayed with generous friends we had met from a previous visit. She and her husband had lived in Anchorage for over thirty years and were wonderful sources of past settlement stories and advice.

Another friend had lived five blocks from me in Florida but we never met. We were introduced by mutual friends and met for the first time in Anchorage! She introduced me to the local botanical gardens where she was a volunteer and included me when she took her daughter to see the local production of *Peter Pan*. These are examples of friendships in Alaska happening easily and naturally.

I met other friends by traveling throughout Alaska. One of my travel destinations was to Bethel, a remote hub of Yupik life on Alaska's west coast. There I met my Native Alaskan friend, Dorothy. During subsequent visits, she and her family invited me to stay in their modest home. We took sweat baths with steam, produced by pouring water over hot rocks. We told each other our life histories. She and her husband and their three children would later come to visit me when I was living in Portland. In Alaska, she shared the fun of picking tiny tundra cranberries. In Portland, I shared the fun of picking corn and blackberries at a local farm.

I met my liveliest and most colorful friend at a drag show with my son. In those days, I was willing to try almost anything! Nina was the sister of one of my son's friends and she was living in Anchorage with her family, far from her

115

CHOOSE TO MOVE

New Jersey roots. Her street-wise wisdom was invaluable as I sorted out what to do next. She had simple philosophies, gusually explained with expletives, that went something like this, "Stop bullshitting around, shit don't come to you, you gotta go find it" or "Put your fucking seatbelt on—you know the police are trying to make money for the governor." When she took up Buddhism, she complained, "Guess I can't go around chanting motherfucker any more!" Her family considered me family and welcomed me whenever I returned to Anchorage. Did I mention this was a Puerto Rican family? In Anchorage, it didn't matter.

At work, which is not always a promising place to find friends, I even made friends. Two colleagues, a short-timer (common in Alaska) and a fifteen-year resident, both gave me rides to work. During one of those rides, we almost hit a moose calf as it crossed a five-lane highway to reunite with its mother on the other side.

At work, I was teased about needing snowshoes to get to work once winter came. They almost convinced me!

In Anchorage showing up, doing what I loved to do, and being patient worked to produce enduring friendships. With work and my son's occasional visits, I wasn't as needy for personal contact and engaging conversation. My expectations were also more realistic for what it takes to make friends.

PORTLAND

Ah, Portland! My skills for making friends really matured there because it was to Portland that I moved *alone*. I had no brother to live with and no son to keep me company. I had no friends to visit. This time I was on my own!

116

The loneliness was real for me those first months in Portland. No lights blinked on my answering machine and no Friday night invitations were offered. I stayed late at work just for the human company and then sought out the soft chairs at the local bookstore. I took long drives alone. I talked to the fish in my aquarium. And I began to know who I was. I redefined friends and family in terms that prospered my life. Out of the loneliness came a whole person. I have never lost that.

The *first friends* principle was originated in Portland because that's where it first happened. I had two really difficult *first friendships*. One was with a woman who did not take care of herself and I often found myself stranded physically and emotionally. Her pent-up anger would surface when plans did not work out, and usually in my direction. But this *first friend* was willing to give me directions, take me shopping, and spend weekends touring me around Portland. The other *first friend* would invite me on extensive trips and go all out to make them happen. We went to a blues festival together when tickets were hard to find. We went to the coast, an hour's drive away, and ate at a fancy restaurant. Then, quite abruptly, she said good-bye, explaining that she was too unstable to be a friend. I suspect it was the commitment part that troubled her. These friendships were mostly painful experiences but they offered me much needed companionship. These *first friends* got me through those first hard months when I was new in town and did not have much to give to a friendship.

One gray, rainy day I took an adult enrichment class about work as spiritual practice. The teacher was to become my mentor. She had a positive outlook and was perfect for this time in my life. We agreed to weekly meetings to review my goals and to sort out my options. Pam has helped me redefine the concept of family and has become family to me over the years of our friendship.

I also found a friend through a class offered by the local recreation department. It was an evening tour of the downtown Portland art galleries. During this tour I met a woman whose interests were art festivals and historical sites. Irene was married and yet glad to find someone with whom to share adventures. We made weekend trips to the beach together, planted vegetables in a community garden plot, and wearily canoed down the Willamette River. She was my first friend in Portland. And our friendship survived. When I moved to Denver and then to Austin, she visited me in those cities.

I met Irene four months after I moved to Portland. That was how long it took for me to show up enough times for meetings to mature into friendships. Knowing this helped me have more realistic expectations about how long this process of finding friends took.

I made short-term friendships with Mexican migrant workers whom I voluntarily taught to speak English. I asked them to tell me about the conditions of their lives. Some of them had wives and children in Mexico whom they had not seen in two years. Others were single and sent money back to aging parents. I conversed with them using my mothball Spanish. However, I was supposed to be letting them practice their English and they often reminded me to "say it in English." I felt camaraderie with them and liked having my social conscience expanded. These friends were only for the hour but knowing them was meaningful.

MAKING FRIENDS

The friends I made at work were also culturally enriching. At Intel, there were many workers from India. I became very interested in their cuisine and culture. While the young men worked, their new brides, also from India, stayed home, isolated from American culture. Here was an opportunity for me to help those I knew. I took these young couples to see fields of pink and yellow tulips and introduced them to the local farmers' market. When one of the families had a baby, I offered my services as an afternoon baby-stroller pusher. The new parents welcomed the break and I enjoyed having a baby to cuddle. I took an Indian wife to a class in interior decorating. We compared our dream homes in our respective cultures and how we would furnish them. The biggest difference was that she would be expected to house her husband's parents!

Some of the brides cooked native foods for me. They showed me how to buy mustard seeds, fennel seeds, and curry mixes at the local Indian food store. Like my tutored friends, these friends were for the hour and they enriched my life.

On an airplane, I met a wheat farmer from The Dalles, a town two hours east of Portland. He operated a large wheat farm he had inherited. My curiosity and genuine interest in his farm led to an invitation to visit. I didn't really believe it was a genuine invitation until I got an e-mail asking which weekend I could come. I named my date and spent a weekend at the farm. I rode in the combine tractor that harvested the ripe grains. His wife Sally and I became very close friends. I visited the farm often. Sally was glad for a visitor to show around, so off we'd go and leave the farmer home to harvest the wheat! If I had not accepted a generous invitation I would have missed

CHOOSE TO MOVE

knowing these resourceful people and missed learning about the wheat-farming business in Oregon.

A birding trip to southeastern Oregon also produced new friends. On that trip I met a couple in their eighties who lived near me in a little town called Hillsboro. After the trip, we continued to see each other. I helped Allen with his computer and, in turn, he and his wife Flo skunked me at games of rummy tiles. We munched on local hazelnuts and occasionally, I even won a game! We also met for pizza at a little haunt in Hillsboro and shopped for asparagus at the Saturday market. Through their stories, I discovered the fascinating history of Hillsboro and its early residents.

I remember one evening when we met for our usual pizza splurge. Afterward, we enjoyed the evening street fair where vendors sold fruits, homemade bread, jellies, and crafts. As we walked back to the car, Allen pointed to an antique store and told how this store used to be a movie theater and a local gathering place. He told me about the newspaper and how, years ago, it gave away newsprint paper to the teachers for school projects. From Allen's recollections, I began to see what this sweet little town had been like in times past.

My friendships in Portland were wonderful! This is the entry from my journal made during the final months in Portland:

To my friends:
I have no community, no permanence, no home right now except myself.
My days are spent in the clearest, purest forms of living—doing what I
enjoy, honoring what I love, sharing with my friends. Where you have
agreed to show up in my life, you have been extraordinary. Thank you.

120

DENVER

In Denver, I had the most relaxed time adjusting and making friends. I had left a stressful job and was taking time to attend graduate school at a Methodist seminary. This school setting practically guaranteed deep, personal involvement. I also had realistic expectations about friends and knew that it would take time, close to four months, before I would find someone compatible for mountain drives or Western art museums. Since I knew friendships would happen, I relaxed and found interesting activities to do on my own. I acquired a gorgeous white cat that kept me company, attended ice hockey games of my coworkers, and volunteered to drive our housing manager to the doctor when she needed a ride.

In Denver, I was reminded of the *first friends* principle. I had *first friends* who would study for exams and discuss God with me. We would take weekend breaks from school by picnicking in the mountains. I noticed who took care of themselves and who didn't. I got a new twist on the *first friends* principle when I was approached by bisexual women at the seminary with offers of more than friendship. I learned to decline their advances and accept their friendship. None of these *first friendships* endured because we had nothing in common outside of school.

It was a delight when friends from other places came to visit. Helen, with whom I had lived in San Diego, actually drove with me from Portland to Denver. A few months later, Irene came from Portland and we drove to Santa Fe to enjoy the orange and red fall colors. And Sally, the wheat farmer's wife, flew to Denver to visit as well!

My massage therapist became a helpful friend. Through the weekly sessions we got acquainted and began to share our interests and life goals. Valerie took me to her yoga class for exercise and introduced me to a women's group who observed Celtic holidays. She took me to a natural hot springs in the mountains where we sat naked and shared our stories. Bethel revisited! When I moved to San Antonio, she and her husband strolled along the River Walk with me. It was Valerie who knew of a house for rent in San Antonio, making that move really easy.

San Antonio

Remember how hard it was for me to make friends the first time in Austin? Remember that the sum total of friends I made was one? My return to Texas was very different. This time, I came with skills for enjoying my circumstances and for making appropriate friends. And make them, I did!

In San Antonio, I rented a house (the one Valerie suggested) in a residential neighborhood of retired people. It was an easy place to make friends, unlike the apartment settings I had been in for the previous few years. I lived next to a couple in their seventies, Elaine and Bill, who also played rummy tiles and didn't skunk me quite so badly. My daytime schedule was flexible since I was telecommuting and could work late at night. Elaine and I would attend new showings at the art museum and I was able to volunteer at Fiesta, a yearly cultural festival, with her. When a flood hit San Antonio shortly after I moved in, they offered comforting reassurance that our houses would not float away!

When I moved back to Austin, an hour's drive away, I still came to visit on weekends. In that way, I could share the events of San Antonio and keep up my rummy-tile skills.

Making friends in San Antonio felt natural and easy. Just like the days of living in Orlando. Maybe I had come full circle in San Antonio.

IN SUMMARY

Today I make friends as naturally as taking a breath. It has been a learned process that took practice and patience. It took showing up and allowing enough time to get to know the other person. The results have all been worth the effort because today I have the most caring, creative friends. They are people who live well and invite me to join them. I also have the most loving family, people who celebrate my life with me and encourage my dreams. Each one is a valuable asset in my life. Each is a special gift from my adventure of moving.

CHOOSE TO MOVE

OTHER QUESTIONS TO THINK ABOUT

1. *Think of one of your very best friends. Remember how you met them. Was it easy or was it hard? Were you doing something you both enjoyed when you met?*

2. *List some qualities you would want in a new first friend.*

3. *List some qualities you would like in a close friend.*

4. *List three activities you enjoy doing with other people. Some suggestions are: eating, watching a movie, shopping, golfing, and walking.*

5. *List three activities you enjoy doing alone. Some suggestions are: reading, exercising, watching TV, and bathing.*

6. *When you want to have fun, what do you do?*

6

Getting Through the Low Feelings

CONSIDER THIS ...

If I could truthfully write this book without talking about loneliness and depression, I would. However, loneliness, sadness, lethargy, and depression are all part of life and in particular, part of moving to a new home. Not talking about theses feelings would be dishonest. These feelings are also part of the work of changing. They will raise a new awareness of yourself and renew your strength for happier times. This is not just fairy-dust wishing, this is the truth.

A group of feelings collectively called depression include sadness, loneliness, lack of joy, lethargy, and anger. Psychologists have spent a lot of time studying why we experience these feelings. You can read their findings in most of the books in the psychology section of any large bookstore. In this book,

CHOOSE TO MOVE

I would like to focus on the remedies—activities and actions that can alleviate the pain caused by these feelings.

Before

I melt in a pool of tears
Surrendering to the fatigue of my situation.
Fully dressed I curl up in a fetal position
And clutch my white fuzzy bear.
God! I'm 54 years old
And all I do is cry,
And remember my dreams—
The house, the truck, the art, the family, the trips, the lover—
None of it comes. None of it.
Why do I keep trying?
Or even keep hoping?
Oh, well—the clothes need to be put in the dryer.

After

Well, yes. 54.
But there's no magic in that number.
Why do I assume I should or could be better?
Curling in a ball is a noble position,
One that lets me flower into a new creation,
Into a second life.
54 is a magic beginning number!

Depression should not be ignored. Serious, deep depression needs to be treated. See a medical physician or health care specialist if you are having severe symptoms, like not being able to get out of bed in the morning or not leaving your house for days at a time. Otherwise, the depression addressed here

GETTING THROUGH THE LOW FEELINGS

robs you of the joy of being alive and keeps you from feeling connected to the world around you.

During a move, we experience the sadness and loneliness of depression. These feelings are expressed in the poem entitled *Before* on the previous page, and the second poem, entitled *After*, expresses the passage through these feelings and a renewed sense of connectedness to life. As the second poem shows, it *is* possible to move through the low feelings to a stronger, healthier outlook of your situation. This is important to remember as you change living places.

WHAT AFFECTS MOOD DURING A MOVE?

Two aspects of moving affect your mood and can't be changed. These are timing and the weather.

Timing

Knowing about the timing for low feelings will help you anticipate them and take actions to dissolve them. Depression is usually most prevalent during the last month before a move and during the first three months after arriving in the new town. I call these varieties departure and arrival depression. Departure depression occurs because you are leaving a place, leaving family and friends, possibly leaving pets, leaving a part of yourself in this place, and leaving a sense of security. There may be fears of the future and sadness from leaving the things you love. Arrival depression begins when you wake up and realize what defined you and what interested you has to be redefined because the town where you just awoke is unfamiliar. In come the loneliness and the sadness from leaving what you loved.

127

Weather

Weather can play a huge part in the way you feel. It affects both your physical and psychological well-being. Getting enough sunshine is one consideration. When you spend days in gray, wet conditions you may get depressed. You can't change the weather but you can change the conditions in your living space. For example, when it is gray outside, go around and turn on all the lights. Light a candle to dispel the gloom. You can decorate with warm colors and soothing patterns from nature, like palm leaves and running water over rocks. When the days are shortened by winter, make sure to get out in the sunlight every day. Plan outings on weekends that are outdoors so that your body will absorb its needed sun energy.

Be aware that weather is an important element to consider when you move.

CHANGING YOUR MOOD

With a little effort, it is possible to change a low mood to a more positive one. Here are more activities and circumstances that may help change your frame of mind. Most of them worked for me, but some didn't. And some won't work for you either. That's okay—all that's needed is one effective action and your mood will be uplifted.

Setting and Accomplishing Goals

Setting a goal and achieving it can go a long way to dispelling the feelings of lethargy and fear that come with depression. Even achieving a very small goal, like getting the dirty clothes washed and folded, will help. Small goals may also include a weekly walk, paying the bills on Thursday, or brushing your teeth before you go to bed. It isn't necessary to have and achieve big goals to make this idea work. In fact, if you set too large a goal and don't achieve it, then you may feel like you aren't making progress at all.

I'm a huge fan of making lists. When I move, or when I feel depressed, I make a list of things I want to accomplish. These are small things like getting flowers for the apartment, reading mail, and taking a walk for half an hour. When I do them I cross them off the list. That gives me a sense of control and movement. The ultimate reward comes when I can toss the completed list gleefully into the trash. Then I know I am really going to make it to the next sunrise!

Hobbies and Interests

If you are a mentally healthy adult over twenty, you have developed interests in your life. You will take these interests with you to your new community. During the adjustment period, they may serve you well. They may be a means to get your feet moving, which is necessary to survive somewhere other than in or under the bed. Although I never have the same passion for my interests during depression as I do otherwise, I do manage to find activities that interest me and are remedies for low feelings when they occur.

In a new location, different resources and opportunities for your interests or hobbies will exist. These resources can be a way of connecting you with your new community. Photography is an example. Most towns have photography clubs that meet monthly. A photography store will know about them. Meeting with a group of people who share your interest is an easy way to find new friends. Go on fieldtrips to photograph the landscape, buildings, or people in your new town. You

CHOOSE TO MOVE

may actually find yourself enjoying your hobby more and minimally, it will get you moving.

In addition you may discover *new* interests. In Portland, I was introduced to glass blowing and the wonderful art created in this way. I began to collect glass pieces and found others who shared my interest. Now it is a hobby I can enjoy as I travel and move.

Learning

What fun learning can be when you are content! And what a diversion it can be when you are depressed! In either case, learning something new is like a trip to explore unfamiliar territories. It's an excellent trip to take when you are just getting adjusted and feeling lonely. Learning may enable you to rise above your present mood and to get a new outlook on your situation. You may also grow in knowledge. And knowledge is power, the power to change and improve your life.

No limits exist for how you can learn. Taking a class is only the most common venue for learning. You can also learn by example when learning a sport, you can learn by doing when learning to draw, you can learn by experiencing when forming a pot, you can learn by being still when you view a bird through the binoculars. You can learn by reading signs at a plant nursery, you can learn by trying a new cuisine, you can learn by the thrill when you take that first glider ride, or you can learn by watching a nature show on PBS. And don't forget about reading! It is a wonderful way to learn. Whatever way you choose, you will be rewarded for having let your mind travel down the unfamiliar information road to discovery.

130

Humor

Everything written about the positive healing effects of humor is true. Humor has a way of healing that allows us to vent the anger and frustration that may accompany a move. It may take some effort, but try to put a large dose of it in your life. When we are able to laugh, we are able to let go of some of the fears and go bravely into this new world that moving provides.

Try finding a funny TV show or radio show. *Car Talk* was the radio program that made me laugh on Saturday mornings. I listen to it in every new town. I am guaranteed a few laughs and a lighter spirit for the next few days.

Variety

Some of us like change and some of us don't. I am a person who likes change, who enjoys going to an unfamiliar restaurant or attending a new church. New activities will relieve my depression for awhile. It may work that way for you, too. You can regulate how much newness is in your life by scheduling one new activity a week, or a month. The possibilities for activities are endless. You can go exploring on your own to an interesting park or shop in a new district. You can try dancing lessons. Or you could take a course at the nearest community college. New people, new surroundings, and new foods can get your mind off your loneliness. And new doors of opportunities will open as well for friends, get-togethers, and interests.

On the other hand, if you need structure and familiarity in your life, then the move itself may be all the newness you can stand. In that case, surround yourself with happy photographs and souvenirs from past trips. Find groups and activities you have enjoyed in the past. You may join a church of your same denomination or join a group that you belonged to in your old hometown, like the Audubon Society or Toastmasters. These are ways to surround yourself with the familiarity you need to thrive.

Exercise

Exercise can be thought of as enjoyable movement of the body. The goal is to get moving in a way that is fun for you. Dancing, swimming, and hiking are some enjoyable ways to move the body. And once the body is moving, it begins to feel real. It has rhythm and warmth and pain and when you experience these, you begin to feel real, too. If you continue to exercise, your body will grow stronger and with that strength will come confidence. Confidence in one's self dispels depression as fast as the snap of a finger.

It always sounds easy and simple, and we know it is not. Physically moving your body is the last thing you may want to do when you feel sad and lonely. I write the words easily but this is not an easy one to follow. Hurray for you if you can muster the discipline to get your body moving at these difficult times. Remember, even the smallest movement like a leisurely walk will lift your spirits.

Support System of Friends and Family

The down times are the times when you will need your strongest support systems. These are the times to splurge on long-distance phone calls. Mentors, old friends, counselors, and anyone who cares about you may become part of your support system. They are able to see beyond this hard time for you. They can label your pain as temporary and can see the brighter days of your future. Perhaps these kind souls are

GETTING THROUGH THE LOW FEELINGS

able to cry with you and they surely can laugh with you. They may have gone down a similar path and know what you are experiencing. They most likely will not be family, although they could be. They most likely will have been in your life for a long time, although they may also be new. They may take pay for their support, or it may be free for the asking.

Social Activities

Activities with other people may also be a cure for your low feelings. You can share a latte, a movie, or a walk in the park. It is a light kind of sharing and perhaps your deeper feelings won't even get discussed. You can join a social group, a church group, a special interest group, or take a class. There will be opportunities to introduce yourself and meet other people. New acquaintances will open up your world to their interests and activities. For someone who is lonely, this can be a good thing. Don't expect too much from this, but do enjoy what comes along.

One important aspect to remember about new activities is that consistency is important. If you are joining a new group *every* week, this can be lonelier than staying home. I recommend groups that meet on a regular basis in order to be with familiar people from week to week. It's being with the same people over a period of time that will give you the feeling of being connected—so important to a cheerful outlook.

Some activities are not usually productive ways to meet people and share time together. These activities include mall shopping, unless you are very gregarious; health clubs, unless you are very confident; going to a movie or eating alone in a restaurant where you will be avoided like the plague; attending art museums; or attending the main worship service of a

133

CHOOSE TO MOVE

church, unless the church is very gregarious. These activities will require extra effort if you are to meet others.

Pets

Whether a pet wards off your depression depends on your attitude and situation. Pets can be a blessing or a nuisance, depending on your own readiness to care for another creature. I believe having a pet is a two-way street; they give affection and you provide good care. If you are not able to provide that care, don't impose yourself on a pet. It just isn't fair to either of you.

One possibility for having a pet that isn't permanent is to be a foster home for stray cats or dogs. They need love and care while in your home. Through an adoption program, they will be placed in a permanent home. If you enjoy pets, but aren't ready for one of your own, or will be moving soon, this may be a workable alternative.

If you are able to give loving care to a pet, then I don't have to write another word about the many advantages of having a pet. You probably know them all!

Journaling

Journaling is really just writing down your thoughts, feelings, and desires. It's saying them, sorting them, dreaming them, and reaffirming the important parts. There are no rules. It's the expressing that is important. From that expressing comes the clarity which is often blurred by loneliness and sadness.

An empowering topic for journaling is the successes that you experience each day. Perhaps you can set a goal of recording three positive things about your day before you go to sleep at night. This is a way to see that your life is going in a positive

134

GETTING THROUGH THE LOW FEELINGS

direction. One of my favorite journaling exercises is to begin my day by writing my wildest desires. This is a sure way to jump-start the day!

Whole sections of bookstores are devoted to journaling and its benefits. Take some time and sit with some of these books to see if this appeals to you. Take a week and journal daily. See if your mood changes or your decisions become easier.

Here is a poem from my journal:

No Happy Poems

A friend asked me for a happy poem.
I don't have any
Because poems are the lifeboats
That rescue me when I'm drowning,
In the black muds of depression.

When I'm happy
I want to be in the water, stay in the water.
I want to be rolled and tossed until I lose my grip
Until I swirl to the very bottom
And rise to the surface again.

Would I climb out onto a bank
With all my ecstasy,
Take up a pen
And limit my joy with mere words?

Giving Back

One of the fastest ways to feel like you are living a worthwhile life, and hence to dispel depression, is to give back to others. You can help those who need comfort, a warm meal, or a listening companion. You can teach English, deliver meals,

135

ferry someone to an appointment, shop for a housebound person, watch a pet, paint a house, or plant a garden. Try giving back in the form of mentoring someone else to realize their dreams. There are always folks who are not as far along as you are. They would benefit from the wisdom you have gained on your journey.

When you can make the world a happier place for someone else, you will begin to realize you have a lot to be grateful for and a lot more gifts to share. I once heard this: "You have sat in the shade of a tree you did not plant and you have drunk from a well you did not dig. Now it is your turn to plant and dig for others."

Achievement

By achieving I mean accomplishing something you can feel proud about. Achieving puts you back in your power. It gives you wings to fly again. It may come at work when you complete a complex task. It may come in your backyard when the first tomato matures after months of nurturing. It may come in your private life when you are told how much your words have meant to someone. Or it may come in the quiet moments of the space with yourself when you realize you have met the goal of healthy eating all day that day. Whatever the accomplishment, it is important because it will increase your sense of mastery of your life. To feel pride and mastery in your life will help overcome the inertia of depression.

Remembering the Purpose for Moving

When the sad, angry, frustrated feelings arise, they hide the real purpose for doing what you are doing. They make you forget why you moved, why you chose this place, and what you want to have in your life. This is when you need to remember your *Life's Essentials* list that we talked about in Chapter 1. Paste the list on a mirror or on the inside cover of your appointments book. Tattoo it on your brain until you have it memorized. Then you can remember what you value and why you are here. Look forward to the future! Don't worry that you don't seem to be making progress. Just keep the destination in sight.

For me, the goal of each move was to be able to embrace each new place and to feel at home anywhere. It was also to have all my hobbies, interests, and values supported and enriched. Those goals have been my driving force to keep me going during the slow times of depression. Depression may be a signal to slow down, but it is not a signal to stop living.

Going Back for a Visit

I want to say a brief word about going back home during the first three months of your move. It has both advantages and disadvantages. Going back may help to alleviate the homesickness you are feeling. It may be just what you need to remember that you *were* connected to a community and will be again. It may also be a reality check that the old place wasn't quite as nice as you remember. In that case, your urge to move back may not be as strong once you go back for a visit. Going back home could bring sadness when you realize the people you left have moved on with their lives and you are no longer a part of that. If you decide to go back home for a visit during the first three months of a new move, be aware of your possible reactions.

Health

Here are some health suggestions. Most of them you have heard before. Rest when you are tired, eat when you are hungry, don't be alone too long, take vitamins, spend time with positive people, and get touched in a loving way once a week. Try a massage. Eat a really special meal once a week. Play daily. Light a candle. In these ways, you are taking care of your body. This is essential for having positive feelings in your life.

Keeping It Light

Don't tackle weighty psychological or emotional activities during the first months of your move. You may be thinking *I don't do weighty psychological or emotional activities*. Let me give you some examples: planning your funeral, writing your will, falling in love, getting another car, making significant financial investments, having an operation, Hospice volunteering, getting married, selling something meaningful, getting a pet, or giving up a pet. The fact is, you just aren't in a clear frame of mind to be making big, emotional decisions. Once you get a support system and settle down, you will be more than able to do these things.

I learned this the hard way shortly after moving to Denver. Five weeks after arriving, I met with an estate planner who asked me numerous life-and-death questions. I saw my whole life pass before me, and all the lives I had not chosen to live. I went home and experienced core grief. Estate planning is too heavy an emotional load to tackle when you have just moved to a new town.

You don't want to experience any more emotional pain than necessary—there is certainly enough already. Keep the decisions light for the first few months.

HOW I DID IT

Oh, can I write about the times of feeling low!! I had my share of them. For me, though, the down times were also the times when I took off my mask, learned who I really was, and developed strength from deep within my soul. In hindsight, these low times were actually blessings.

AUSTIN

Austin was my first attempt to move alone and it was very hard. I called friends back in Florida almost daily, often in tears. They were my support system, encouraging me while I spouted frustrations and disappointments. I had the largest telephone bills of my life during those first months in Austin!

I tried to meet people by doing the same activities I had done in Florida. I attended meetings of the Audubon Society and the Native Plant Society. With Audubon, I went hiking and participated in my first bird banding. With the Native Plant Society, I enjoyed the wildflower trails and the limestone outcroppings of the Texas Hill Country.

Since I had been a Hospice volunteer in Florida, I volunteered for Hospice in Texas. After weeks of training I was beginning to know the other volunteers, but I didn't initiate activities with anyone and therefore, didn't make a friend this way.

I also started a new hobby, geology. I joined a group of geologists who took trips and gave lectures. I learned about the unique rock formations in this part of Texas. As a result, rock collecting is an enjoyable hobby.

CHOOSE TO MOVE

Springtime in Texas unveils a rainbow of wildflowers—red, orange, pink, white, and blue. I made them the subjects of my landscape photographs, continuing a beloved hobby with new subject matter. Once, I set up my tripod next to a picturesque limestone wall and took photos for hours. During these photography sessions, I experienced total surrender to my art and escaped my loneliness.

Despite these efforts, I moved back to Florida. I didn't know enough remedies to move through the depression and to be able to adjust in a new community.

ANCHORAGE

The next time I left Florida, all my belongings stayed behind except my clothes. I took the best antidote for depression—my dear, adult son. He drove to Anchorage and stayed on after I left. Friends helped us get settled. This move was undoubtedly the happiest of all the ones I made. Any depression I experienced was quickly dispelled by fun activities and warm friendships.

Since the geology group had been a fun and stimulating group in Austin, I joined a similar group in Anchorage. The Anchorage geology club went gold hunting and geode collecting. Some members were actual miners and I listened to exciting tales of scouting for hidden gold.

In Florida, I had been an avid birder. In Anchorage, I joined a local chapter of the Audubon Society and viewed the migratory birds that came through this part of the North. I saw Northern pintail ducks, sandhill cranes, and black-capped chickadees. The funny part was that we saw birds in May as they went north and again in August when they went south. Summers are short if you are a migratory bird in Alaska!

140

GETTING THROUGH THE LOW FEELINGS

I began a new hobby of buying art from Native Alaskan artists who lived in the area. These were items made from animal and plant parts, like feathers and bark. When I brought a new art acquisition home to my nearly empty apartment, the piece transformed my place into a castle filled with beautiful treasures.

The presence of wild animals made living in Anchorage very exciting. I soon forgot my loneliness when a moose crossed the main highway or when salmon spawned in the local streams. I once had to wait inside a grocery store until a large moose left the parking lot. These new elements in my life kept me upbeat and curious.

I began to journal the events of my life and my feelings about them. This made me aware of how I was feeling moment to moment. One time, while I was driving in downtown Anchorage, the thought came to me that I was so happy and this was the best it was going to get for me. When I recorded it that night, I began with, *"This is as good as it gets ..."* and wrote about the experience. Through the years, I have maintained this ritual of recording special times when life is as good as I could ever want it to be. Each entry begins, *"This is as good as it gets ..."*

During my stay, I made many adjustments. My bed consisted of an inflatable mattress on the hard floor and I was living in a shabby neighborhood. I didn't have my beloved art or my comfortable chairs. My friends were four time zones away. My son had his own life. Occasionally earthquakes moved the landscape. Ten-foot tall moose impeded the paths. The roads got icy and the weather turned cold and dark in the fall. I adjusted to it all!

141

CHOOSE TO MOVE

PORTLAND

Portland was the proof of my ability to move and to be successful. I had never even been to that city, or to Oregon, when I made the decision to move. All I had was a job offer and my moving skills. To adjust in Portland, I used *all* the coping activities we have discussed. I needed them all!

It was here I suffered the worst depression —weather was one of the biggest causes. For nine months of the year, gray skies blocked out the sunshine. Rain was the usual fare; in addition, local people appeared remote and uncaring. My work environment was fast-paced and confrontive. The final blow to my resilience came when my beloved red sports car I had owned for twelve years died from the Oregon unregulated gasoline I fed it. Who wouldn't have been depressed? I became lonely, incredibly sad, and very angry.

For the first time, I used humor to get me through the low feelings. Every Saturday morning I tuned in faithfully to *Car Talk* on the radio and laughed out loud as I drove. One time, I laughed so hard I had to pull over to the side of the road and stop. Click and Clack were reading the menu of the Road Kill Café. I also watched British comedies on the local PBS station. Mr. Bean kept me entertained in the evenings with his outrageous antics.

October Activites
- Civil War re-enactment
- apple festival
- wine country tour
- Lewis and Clark fort
- fly-fishing course
- cherries ripening
- apples ripening
- history lecture at the museum

In order to get myself out on the weekends, I developed an activities schedule. I wrote down interesting events and desired destinations on a card, one card for each

142

month of the year. Ripening dates for each crop were also listed on the appropriate card.

As the weekend approached, I would pull the card for that month and choose two or three ideas from it. In this way, I had structure for my solitary weekends and I participated in community events and activities.

My favorite outing was to visit the fruit and vegetable crops that grew everywhere. I picked strawberries, blackberries, boysenberries, loganberries, peaches, pears, hazelnuts, cherries, plums, corn, apples, and even a pumpkin fresh from the field for Halloween. I saw corn growing for the first time, I walked among three varieties of apple trees in one yard, and I cut fresh sunflowers for my kitchen. Each time I visited a farm, my low feelings would vanish. It was a love affair for me, all this fresh, growing stuff.

I enjoyed the produce so much that I rented a plot in a community garden and grew tomatoes, zucchini, dill, arugula, green beans, and snow peas. I also tried potatoes at the urging of another gardener but they never came up.

I also volunteered, teaching English as a Bravo Volunteer to Mexican migrant workers. I really enjoyed learning about their lives and how they existed alone while their families were in Mexico. I joined the local PBS station and answered phones during membership drives. It was an easy way to meet others on an informal, fun basis. When I was giving of myself, I was never depressed.

Reading was a favorite diversion when the rain prevented outside activities. In Portland, I discovered the soft, overstuffed chairs at Barnes and Noble and found them to be comforting curatives for the damp, gray mess outside. I read for hours and made the acquaintance of many fine books. I could have made the acquaintance of fine people as well if I had tried.

I enrolled in classes at the local community college and the neighborhood recreation center. They included fly-fishing, cooking with apples, beading, gyoto fish painting, Native American art history, and travel tips. I even dabbled in personal growth classes like work as a spiritual practice, how to meet a partner, and living simply.

Oregon and the Willamette Valley were at the end of the Oregon Trail. That heritage was preserved in old fort sites, stately houses of early settlers, and worn covered-wagon trails in the mountains. The covered wagons could almost be heard squeaking to a halt and setting up house just over the next hill. History was everywhere and I took an interest in it. I read biographies and visited historical sites. These learning activities stimulated and enriched me as well as kept me from sinking into depression.

My dream during this time was having my own place in a sunny climate. So I built a balsa-wood model of the home I hoped to build someday. It was a 3-D rendition complete with stairs, windows, and a landscaped yard. I also began to write. It became a way to get outside the feelings of loneliness and sadness. It helped me remember why I had moved to Oregon— to find the magic in this place and make it my home.

For emotional reinforcements, I made two folders for myself. One was labeled *You Are Not Alone* and the other was labeled *Life Is Fun*. I filed comforting sayings, friends' greeting cards, and things that made me laugh in these folders. When I got depressed I would sit on my fuzzy, forest green sofa, open these folders and read. I would remember the positive things in my life, and would feel connected again. Lighting a candle added a warm ambiance to the occasion.

I acquired a young male cat for company, found a massage therapist in the Yellow Pages, recruited the teacher of a self-help class as my mentor, and began taking the herbal supplement St. Johns wort for emotional equilibrium. The list of the remedies I used to survive and to thrive in Portland is long. They all worked, and that's all that matters!

DENVER

Moving to Denver was easier than moving to Portland. I had visited Denver on vacation trips and I knew my way around. It was also easier because I attended graduate school at a seminary. The school provided an immediate community connection. And finally, it was easy because the ability to adjust after a move gets strengthened by use. After four moves, I had that ability in spades!

This was an introspective period of my life. I used journaling to look back and feel pride about the moves I had made and about my freedom to move again. I actually did a lot of writing during this move, completing assignments for classes and editing this book. When I needed a change of pace, I ran away in my truck to interesting places like Santa Fe or Vale. Especially in the fall, the driving was fabulous with the aspen trees turning shades of red and orange, and the cottonwood trees dropping their yellow leaves in anticipation of winter.

I carried a full load of academic classes at the seminary. I studied social injustices in our country, pastoral counseling, and managing change in the workplace. After class, more discussions and heated debates ensued about our individual roles in changing the society. We argued about whether America was a Christian country and why the gap was widening between the rich and the poor. For relief from these heavy issues, I escaped to Tattered Cover Bookstore and read for fun. I also found a wonderful masseuse who un-kinked my stiff neck muscles—from too much reading.

The altitude and the weather definitely influenced my moods. The atmosphere was thin at five thousand feet. I had to breathe a lot and get extra rest until I got accustomed to the air pressure. I walked every chance I got. I found little parks and lakes near my dormitory that lifted my spirits. I paced my walks and measured the distance to feel like I accomplished something. I actually lost weight, which boosted my self-esteem. And no, I never learned to ski!

In the winter, I rode the bus to my downtown job. Sometimes while I waited at the bus stop, the snow would start to fall. I would pull my jacket hood closer around my face and smile inwardly to myself. Here I was, fifty-something, experiencing my first winter in snow and doing it out in public with all the other bus riders of Denver. For me, these were significant accomplishments. They helped me overcome feelings of confinement and powerlessness in the face of winter weather.

Six months after I arrived, a spring blizzard dropped twenty inches of snow in two days. Because I was not accustomed to these weather conditions, I bought extra groceries when the radio advised it. Housebound, I wrote *My First Blizzard*.

This move was different because I started earlier to do healthy activities. I didn't experience the prolonged or deep depression I had experienced in Portland. By this move, I was conscious of what I needed to do and what would work for me.

GETTING THROUGH THE LOW FEELINGS

My First Blizzard

It snowed and snowed and snowed and snowed
All day yesterday and the day before.
I watched through a little peephole in my window blinds
As trees turned white and streets disappeared
Then it stopped snowing.
Today the sun is back.
I watch the three icicles on a bare branch
Drip and grow shorter
I laugh as limbs drop their snow bombs on cars below
And trees have their skirts down around their ankles
And water streams form wriggly snakes through the white,
icy mush.

I'm a little kid again about to discover new things
As I put on three layers and unfamiliar snow boots.
Cautiously I go out into the wind and cold fluff
Putting one foot down to firm ground and then the other,
A coolness in my toes.
I move forward totally in love.
They called it a blizzard. I call it my first snow love affair.
- Denver

I exercised, had out-of-town friends come to visit, pursued my art-collecting hobby, sought out learning experiences, listened to *Car Talk* on the radio, and journaled. I began a new activity when I joined the Mustang Owners Club, a group of people who drove and adored Ford Mustang cars.

I moved past the arrival depression more quickly and thrived emotionally within the first few months in my new community.

147

IN SUMMARY

There are many ways to uplift your mood. Try whatever brings you joy and comfort. But don't try too hard. This is a time for slowing down and for adjusting to new circumstances. Once the adjustment is made in a few months, the low feelings will likely pass.

OTHER QUESTIONS TO THINK ABOUT

1. *Do you know when you need to park your activities temporarily and refuel emotionally?*

2. *When you are lonely, how do you fill the time?*

3. *How quickly can you recover from a down period? Can you experience the down feelings and move on or do the feelings stay for days?*

4. *Name three people you could call for support. Name one person you could call in the middle of the night.*

5. *Have you ever volunteered for a worthy cause? Did you enjoy the experience?*

6. *Name three positive changes you have made in the last year.*

7. *When you need fresh flowers, where do you go to buy them? If you were in a new town where would you go?*

Part Three

SEEING HOW FAR YOU'VE COME

7

Expanding Your Territory

CONSIDER THIS ...

Now we can talk about expanding your territory with new experiences. These new experiences may be exploring new towns and tasting new foods. They may be trying new hobbies and seeing new sights. The opportunity to experience interesting places, activities, people, and food is one of the best payoffs for moving to a new community. These experiences may enlarge your set of friends, abilities, hobbies, cuisine, and knowledge of your new surroundings.

A move will have elements to it that are unfamiliar, some expected and some not. The expected ones, like the weather or the population, are probably why you chose this town as home in the first place. The unexpected ones, like the friendliness of the people or the variety of food selections, will be pleasant bonuses!

CHOOSE TO MOVE

> *And I think over again*
> *My small adventure*
> *Traveling alone*
> *Over new ground*
> *Thinking I was in danger.*
> *My fears*
> *Those I thought so big*
> *For all the vital things*
> *I had to get and to reach*
> *And yet, there is only*
> *One great thing: Living.*
> *(Adapted from an Eskimo poem)*

Throughout my moves, I chose places for the weather or for the cultural advantages of museums and festivals. Sometimes I just wanted a larger, or a smaller, town to call home. I was expecting these differences. However, it was all the *unexpected* new things that I experienced, which made moving so amazing for me. It was the beautiful light in Denver that made colors brighter and clearer. It was the Mexican festivals with Mariachi music and fish tacos that made San Antonio a pleasant surprise. And it was the warmth of the people in Anchorage that made that town so special.

I encourage you to go for the gusto every time: try it, do it, see it. Expanding your territory can be fun!

NEW TERRITORY TO EXPLORE

As soon as you can, drive around and see what's in your new locale. One way to go exploring is to find nearby places that are interesting and go visit. Make these early explorations within an hour's drive and you can enjoy the outing without getting too tired. To find these special-interest spots, use the newspaper, visitors' information center, local bookstore, library, or ask around. Wildlife areas, gardens, ghost towns, old fort sites, shopping malls, beaches, or scenic drives may be close by. If you go alone, find an entertaining radio station for company. You can pack some interesting munchies or have

152

EXPANDING YOUR TERRITORY

bread and cheese by a river or lake. Or plan to find a local restaurant for lunch.

Take a new friend along on a driving trip. It may be a chance for you to get to know each other better. One person may be a birder and the other person an art enthusiast. This could be a fun trip—plan the trip to accommodate both interests. For example, take back roads and go slow enough to look for birds; then drive on to the next town where you could visit art galleries on the main street. A picnic lunch would be a fun addition.

Or, if you don't quite have your adventuring legs under you yet, join a tour group to see the area. Let the leader explain the history and sights. Others in the group may be newcomers, too, or out-of-towners. You may even meet someone from your hometown and get caught up on the news. When you talk to locals after the trip, don't be surprised to discover they haven't visited these places. We often don't go sightseeing in our own backyards!

Nearby towns and cities will also be interesting to experience. These towns may not be your top priority, but since they are closer, visiting them will be cheaper and easier. Take advantage of these opportunities. Use your free days to visit out of town—it's a clever way to have a mini-vacation!

When I was in Portland, I traveled the length of Vancouver Island and spent time in Seattle. From Florida, these places would have been too far to visit. Being in Portland, however, made them accessible. When I was in Denver, I was a few hours from Vale, six hours from Santa Fe, and three hours from Cheyenne. I took advantage of this and visited them all. In San Antonio, I was a day's trip away from Monterrey, Mexico, and

153

CHOOSE TO MOVE

arranged a weekend trip to visit its markets and mountains. In Alaska, I drove or flew to faraway places like Denali and Katmai National Parks, Fairbanks, and Nome.

NEW INTERESTS AND ACTIVITIES TO TRY

In a new community, opportunities will exist to pursue new hobbies, develop new skills, and learn new information. These are avenues for expanding your territory, and occasions to have immense fun. There may be occasions to fly-fish, water ski, snorkel, hear the latest jazz music, dance the hula, dig for clams, or even pick fresh berries. The range of opportunities will be unique to the area and you should take advantage of as many as your sense of adventure allows! You certainly do not have to become a pro—just experiment and see what you like. If you are new to an area, anonymity will be on your side as well. You won't care who sees you because you don't know anyone yet!

Seek out what makes this new community unique and special. This involves asking questions, reading the local newspaper for local events, and getting acquainted. The discoveries you make will take you down some exciting new paths.

Are winter recreational areas nearby? There may be a chance to learn to ski. Is this an area of rich farmlands? Vegetables and fruit may be abundant. Farmers' markets will be available as well as classes on cooking the local produce. Is this an area of the country steeped in history? Bookstores will have diaries of the pioneers and historical sites will be preserved. The unique aspects of a place will be interesting opportunities for growing and learning.

154

EXPANDING YOUR TERRITORY

There are other ways to develop new interests. A formal class may be the way to get started. Hobby classes are held at art stores, recreation centers, fairs, and community colleges. The non-credit programs for adults at universities and high schools offer evening classes on many popular topics.

New interests may also develop from attending cultural events in the town. Music, art, theater, craft fairs, and sports events may stimulate and grow your interests. Museums, cultural centers, plays, and holiday festivals may open new worlds of enjoyment and entertainment. In Denver, for example, wonderful collections of Western art were displayed in local museums. Three professional sports teams had strong local support. Seeing the art and attending the games expanded my interests and knowledge of this town. Portland is becoming the center for Native American art. Each year a national craft fair is held to showcase the leading Native American artists. Cinco de Mayo parades in San Antonio are a highlight of spring, as well as festivals with their succulent Mexican foods. Austin has an active Medieval music society that performs in local churches. Every town has arts and crafts fairs where local artists sell to the public. Every town has a museum filled with local history. And every town has a team that excels in a local sport.

My policy has been to try many activities and keep only the ones I enjoy. For example, I took a class to make clay beads in Denver. The bead creations were gorgeous, but I didn't have the patience to do the intricate design work. I don't make beads today. On the other hand, I tried some activities and really enjoyed them. I now collect handmade fishing flies because I took a fly-fishing class in Portland. From that class I admired the flies and how artistically they were made. I now

155

CHOOSE TO MOVE

collect them in towns where I travel. They are a permanent part of my art collection and wonderful reminders of places I have visited.

NEW PEOPLE TO MEET

I always meet new people when I move; they are friends I just haven't yet bumped into! The same will be true for you. Initial meetings take time to develop into friendships. Perhaps these new acquaintances share some of your interests. They may be younger, older, from a different culture than your own, minorities, disadvantaged, or from your home state. They may have differing sexual preferences or differing religious beliefs from your own. Be open to what each person has to share with you. Remember, you don't have to totally embrace their ways to enjoy having them in your life.

New people can expand your outlook, understanding, and enjoyment of daily life. The wives of my Arabic coworkers taught me how to cook and enjoy Arabic food. Other coworkers were ice hockey players and I attended my first ice hockey games. I lived in a retirement neighborhood in San Antonio where my neighbors shared food and plant cuttings. My moves were enriched from knowing these people, and your move will be enriched, too, by the people you meet.

NEW FOODS TO ENJOY

Think of red and yellow curries, fresh basil and pine nut pesto, mango drinks, tacos filled with fresh fish and cilantro, garlic spreads, fresh rosemary bread, and homemade peach ice cream. Trying new foods can be a sensuous adventure! It's one of the aspects of moving you will really enjoy.

156

Every region has its local food choices and methods of preparation. These include spicy salsas and outdoor barbecues in Texas, grilled fresh salmon in the Northwest, and Cajun cooking in the South. In addition, various cultures that have settled in the area will influence the local food offerings. For example, in Austin and San Diego, the Mexican influence brings boisterous music and spicy foods to every street corner. In Portland the East Indian restaurants with their brick-oven-baked breads are fabulous. The Greek and Vietnamese presence in Denver makes traditional foods available in outlying Denver neighborhoods. Everywhere in every town, wonderful food treats are waiting to be savored.

To find the best places for these new cuisines, ask for recommendations from colleagues and friends. Invite them to come along, too! It will be more fun to go with people who know the directions and know what to order from the menu.

A cultural festival is another place to share local cuisines, crafts, and ethnic music. This can be an entertaining as well as a tasty way to sample new recipes and ingredients. Local restaurants may serve specialty dishes in individual portions so that you can try more than one tempting dish.

HOW I DID IT

The following stories show how changing places has happily expanded the territory of my life. The rewards of new friends, hobbies, and knowledge are enormous. I am so rich today in memories, skills, and experiences for having driven the roads, met the people, and seen the sights.

AUSTIN

Ladybird Johnson started her wildflower campaign in Austin, the state capital. As a result, highways and parks are covered in spring blossoms, one of the unique aspects of Austin. Wildflowers are everywhere! I relished this colorful landscape. I saw unbelievably beautiful spreads of red and yellow Indian blankets, purple bluebonnets, white Mexican poppies, and orange sunflowers. Often I didn't drive more than thirty minutes before I was rewarded with scenes that made me stop the car for a "Kodak moment." On longer drives, I passed through quaint, small towns. Sometimes I packed a lunch before I left home, got a drink or dessert in the town, and made a day of driving and photographing wildflowers.

Austin is also unique for its limestone formations and hilly countryside. I joined the geology society to learn more about these features. I had two enlightening outings, one on a chartered bus with a catered lunch to look at rock strata in the Texas Hill Country, and one to an active anthracite mine. On the bus rides, I began asking questions about the early days of Austin. In this way, I learned how Austin had grown from a banking center for cattle ranchers to being the state capital. Some society members were retired geologists with amazing stories to share about the early oil days.

The longest trip I made beyond Austin was to Big Bend National Park. The park is on the Texas-Mexico border and very far from anywhere else outside of Texas. Living in Austin made the park accessible to me. I traveled with a nature tour from Austin, through San Antonio to Big Bend, through the Davis Mountains, and ended in El Paso. In this way, I got to see a lot of a *very* big state!

158

In Austin I learned what *real* Mexican food is—at least what real Tex-Mex cuisine is—and it is wonderful! Fresh tortillas are made in the local grocery stores or on street corners of Mexican neighborhoods. I discovered the herb cilantro and three new kinds of peppers, not all of them hot. I fell in love with dishes like tortilla soup and cheese quesadillas, now regular additions to my home menus. I enjoyed the Mexican influence with its bright pottery, lively music, and colorful cotton clothing. I attended Mexican festivals to celebrate Independence Day, Day of the Dead, and any excuse to come together to have fun. I usually went alone because in the early days of relocating, I didn't think to ask others to join me. I hadn't yet acquired that skill.

Austin is also a major venue for country music. I tried it even though I was not a fan. I programmed my car radio for local stations and listened to the latest ballads. I also learned the latest line dances in Austin. They were a fun way to exercise and another experience of Texas culture. These days, I no longer program my car radio for country-western music. I do, however, go country-western dancing occasionally. Some new things are keepers while others are only enjoyed for a time.

GAINESVILLE

When I assure you it is safe to try new things because no one knows you, I mean that. In Gainesville I tried something daring. I wanted to experience freedom from wearing clothes in public. So, I visited my first nudist camp! A gorgeous man wearing no clothes gave me a tour of the camp. When I accepted the invitation to spend the day, I asked where I should undress. His answer was, "Anywhere you want to." I didn't

CHOOSE TO MOVE

set any records for walking around, but I did disrobe and enjoy the adventure. It was liberating to try a nudist camp in total anonymity.

I went to Gainesville to work at a state university. My coworkers were in their twenties and I listened to their views of life. Sometimes my own view shifted because of what they shared. I attended seminars where I learned why songbirds are declining in the Appalachian Mountains, how the Everglades are forever ruined, and ways to increase citrus production. I developed an interest in the global effects of reforestation. My environmental perspective was informed from this university setting.

ANCHORAGE

Just going to Anchorage was expanding! The majestic scenery and the Native Alaskan culture were so unique that anyone would be changed who visited. For me, this was a chance to see as many places as time and money would allow. I knew I would probably *never* visit some of these places again once I. returned to the Lower Forty-Eight.

And the trips! I made many excursions throughout Alaska and often I went alone. I went to Katmai National Park by myself and shared trails with the local mob of grizzlies. I also went to Barrow and walked through the streets built on permafrost. Here, local residents displayed drying polar bear skins on front porches. Barrow's beach had entire bowhead whale skeletons and the local kids rode all-terrain vehicles to buy milk at the one and only grocery store. I went to Bethel and was taken by boat to an outlying Yupik community. Its ten miles of paved roads went nowhere. *Steel Magnolias* was the current play in town.

160

Eric, my son, and I made an exciting trip along the Haul Road to Prudoe Bay where the Alaskan pipeline begins. We also won the lottery to drive our own vehicle into Denali National Park. It was an opportunity to view the grizzly bears and caribou to our heart's desire from the comfort of our car. These trips were adventure at its best.

I also visited places closer to Anchorage. I hiked the John Knowles Trail that followed the shoreline of the city, watching out for moose. I joined the Sierra Club and hiked with them into the mountains. That first upward climb is still a poignant memory for me. Coming from Florida, I had never hiked *uphill*. There I was, huffing and puffing the whole way! What I never quite conquered was the fear of a bear encounter. On that hike (and subsequent ones) my feet left the path every time someone stepped on a twig and made it snap. This was definitely not an issue back in Florida.

I joined a geology society and learned about the gold-mining history of Alaska. Geodes, fossil dinosaur eggs, and silver ore samples were brought for display. We once celebrated the birthday of a ninety-five-year-old gold miner!

With the local Audubon Society, I went birding. When the migratory seabirds made their spring and fall trips through the area we were busy observers. In Homer, I met Ann Weiland, a woman who was a persuasive leader in establishing a sea life refuge and a songbird habitat on the Kenai Peninsula. We stayed in her home overlooking the stormy Gulf of Alaska, and visited the sites she had helped to preserve.

New foods were part of my Alaskan adventure. I experienced fresh bread bakeries, tasted whale meat, discovered garlic black-bean sauce, and sampled my first Asian pear.

Choose To Move

Salmon was abundant and grilled to perfection. Blackberries grew in profusion in the summer along with salmonberries and boysenberries.

My art collection began to include Native art that was produced locally. Inupiak and Inuit artists depicted wolves, whales, bears, and moose using white and tan ivory, bleached whale bone, caribou antler, polar bear fur, and black baleen from bowhead whales. I often met the Native artist. Once, in the gift store of the Native hospital, I met a young Inuit male, about twenty. He came in with a large bundle wrapped in brown paper under his arm. He approached one of the clerks and showed her a beautiful, hand-carved, brown wooden kayak with two ivory figures. One was the hunter with his harpoon raised above his head and the other was the captured seal riding on the bow. The clerk declined to buy the piece and I offered to pay what he was asking. I also asked to meet the artist who was the young man's uncle. He took me outside to an elderly man with a richly wrinkled face. When his young nephew conveyed my admiration in Inuit, the old man was very pleased. I felt honored to have met him.

Another time, I liked a poster by a local artist. I found his number in the phone book and called to ask if he had originals for sale. Humbly, he agreed to meet me in the parking lot of the local Subway shop. When he arrived, he had a large leather binder filled with various canvases. I bought several of his grizzly bear paintings. We became friends and have stayed in touch.

I was thrilled to have the opportunity to view and purchase original art in this way. Native Alaskan art is a happy reminder of my days in Anchorage.

PORTLAND

The farmlands surrounding downtown Portland have some of the most beautiful scenery in the world. Apple, peach, and pear orchards cover the sloping hillsides. Mature wheat fields appear as golden patches in a green countryside quilt. Majestic Mt. Hood and Mt. Saint Helens can be seen on the horizon, often with white patches of snow on top. I felt a strong attraction to the land and made many trips into the nearby countryside. At first, I went with a touring company that emphasized ecological awareness. We visited vineyards that didn't spray the grapes and also recycled grape skins. We toured an Indian reservation that captured and trained wild horses. Soon, I was touring on my own. I drove scenic routes, stopped at valley overlooks, and ate lunches beside waterfalls. I became a regular listener of public radio as I drove because weekend programming offered laughter, Celtic music, and news from Lake Woebegone. Other times a friend kept me company. These drives were my way of exploring the unique features of Portland.

I also visited scenic places farther away from Portland. I ventured over the Coast Range Mountains to the Pacific Coast of Oregon. Large rocks called sea stacks line the shore. My introduction to them was with a geology club, of course!

The bus rolls on
Through light-filtering maples
And dark Douglas firs
Sunlight and shadows
Rock road embankments
Snow-covered mountains
Soft-humming engine.
Here I sit writing
Shoulders sun-warmed,
Still wearing my new straw hat.
I am an explorer of the world around me
Feeling alive with joy.

CHOOSE TO MOVE

I drove the length of Vancouver Island with my friend Helen from San Diego. I took a tour with an Audubon Society group to the southeastern part of Oregon where dry desert conditions dominate. I drove the length of the Oregon seaside coast with a friend, and I drove from Portland to Idaho through the breathtaking Columbia Gorge.

Fruits and vegetables were abundant in the area. I especially liked the concept of u-pick, where I went into the fields or orchards and picked my own produce. I studied the cooperative farm bulletin to know where the crops I wanted to pick grew. When the crop I wanted was ripe, I was ready. Often I took a small sack and a large camera, more intent on capturing the beauty of the place than on filling my freezer. This is the long list of produce I picked—Jonathon apples, Granny Smith apples, Bing cherries, Queen Ann cherries, romaine lettuce, pumpkins, filberts, Marionberries, blueberries, raspberries, strawberries, blackberries, boysenberries, peaches, sugar peas, green beans, corn, yellow sunflowers, red poppies, multi-colored tulips, and pink statice.

In the wintertime I visited a Christmas tree farm and walked among eight different kinds of green, stately evergreen trees. I did not have the heart to cut one so I contented myself with smelling the fragrant evergreen oils.

When I wasn't out picking produce on a farm, I was at a local farmers' market. I discovered many new foods—arugula (a type of lettuce), Yukon gold potatoes, lemon-flavored honey, elephant garlic, garlic sprouts, yellow squash blossoms, orange beets, leeks, and fennel bulbs. In addition to the fruits and vegetables, huge sunflowers, multi-flowered bouquets, fresh bread, fruit pies, muffins, goat cheese, locally produced wines,

164

and live plants were for sale. Live music was performed by retirees for donations. It was heaven on earth one day a week!

With a friend, I rented a plot in a community garden surrounded by wheat fields. We divided the plot into eight sections, bought plants and seeds of the vegetables we wanted to grow, and went to work! In less than six weeks we were harvesting zucchini and later tomatoes, corn, cucumbers, onions, sunflowers, sugar peas, green beans, dill, cilantro, green peppers, basil, parsley, carrots, and mint. All in a twenty-by-thirty-foot plot! We had so much to harvest we opened the garden for other friends to enjoy.

Oregon and nearby Washington state have strong historical features. British and Americans carved up this territory for their respective countries. I visited old forts and campsites settled by Lewis and Clark. History has never been a favorite subject, but in Oregon I found it interesting, alive, and personal.

What a bounty of new, unique experiences I discovered in Portland! I went from never having been to Oregon, to embracing the unique wonders of the area in two short years. That's expanding!

DENVER

The most challenging change for me during my stay in Denver was to attend university again. It wasn't an ordinary university, but a seminary for training religious workers. I enrolled in social issues classes, read lots of religious books, slept in late, reassessed my career, and finished the rough draft of this book. From my second-floor apartment, I had a full view to the west of the jagged peaks of the Rocky Mountains. Sunsets were spectacular! The irony was that I was a lowly

165

CHOOSE TO MOVE

graduate student in modest student housing and had this fantastic view! The time at seminary was a tremendously productive and rewarding time for me. It was not an easy change to make and after one semester of full-time studies, I got a job and took classes on a part-time basis. Working was easier than studying and having an income again felt secure. Some expansions are just not the best direction, and we simply re-adjust.

My health improved in Denver, too. After my body got used to the thinner atmosphere, I kept an active schedule. I walked to catch a bus everyday when I worked downtown. I attended lectures on holistic health and bodywork. I had fantastic massages and went to a hot springs spa where I could disrobe and relax.

I made huge adjustments to city life while in Denver. This small town female learned to ride public transportation on a daily basis and learned to work downtown in a large city. I learned to trust myself in crowds and to not sit in the handicap section of the bus. I learned to keep myself safe by walking on lighted streets after dark and by asking for a ride home when it was snowing. I survived without a vehicle in Denver!

I learned to cope with winter weather. I experienced my first blizzard and was thrilled. I learned to walk on snow and ice-covered sidewalks. I bought clothes that kept me warm. When I left Denver, I knew I could live almost anywhere regardless of the winter weather. This was a huge achievement for a person who grew up in Florida!

IN SUMMARY

Expanding your territory involves many facets: exploring your new locale, trying new activities and adventures, meeting new people, discovering new foods and cultures, and much more. Often it's the surprises—the unexpected aspects of a move—which may prove to be the most enriching and life-expanding.

OTHER QUESTIONS TO THINK ABOUT

1. *What does the word adventure invoke in you? Adrenaline rush? Joy? Caution?*

2. *Do you welcome or avoid change?*

3. *Name the most significant change you have made in the last year.*

4. *Name the proudest achievement of your life.*

5. *Name one major change you would like to make in the next six months.*

6. *Name a new food you've tried, a new place you've visited, or a new interest you've acquired in the last three months.*

8

The Incredible Rewards of Moving

CONSIDER THIS ...

The water is lapping at the pilings of the cabana here on Spanish Bay Caye in Belize. I have come to snorkel with my friend Irene. We have a Hawaiian newspaper spread out on the bed, a gift from my friend. We are reading it to see if we want to move there. Five years ago I could not have imagined such an event. Now I am considering moving to a town where I know no one and have no job. Yet it would be a wonderful experience if that is what I decide to do. I know how to do this. I have the skills to do it. I have a friend who will dream with me and might come, too. Opportunities, skills, friends, dreams—these are some of the gifts the last five years of moving have given me.

That was an entry I made in my journal toward the end of writing this book. I share it because it illustrates one reward of moving.

Moving can transform your life. It's like having a door into another life. When Irene and I were sitting in that cabana and dreaming, it was fun to see ourselves in Hawaii, living new adventures. We were creating another life in our dreams. It was exciting and scary at the same time. Dreams can become reality! That's just one reward of moving.

UNIQUE REWARDS

Everyone who moves will reap profound rewards. And everyone's rewards will be different. Each of us will experience areas of our lives that will get strengthened and each of us will have special joys when we pack our bags and move to a new town.

The rewards for moving are different because we each move for different purposes. Some moves are for economic reasons. Some moves are to be closer to family. And some moves are made just because we want to live in another place. This was the rationale for most of my own moves. I moved to enjoy the natural settings of Portland, Anchorage, and Denver. However, for someone else who moves for a job or family, the rewards may be different. Instead of having fantastic scenery, they may enjoy an increased income or seeing grandchildren grow up.

What you recognize as rewards for moving depends on what is important in your life. For some, it's friends and loved ones that make all the difference. For others, it's the beauty in their surroundings. And for others, it's the avenues of personal growth through learning or recreation that are important. You tend to focus your energies, time, and money in the areas that matter the most. The rewards will usually come in these valued areas, too, because they are cultivated the most and enjoyed the most.

Everyone has expectations about what benefits they will get from moving. I expected to see more scenery, make new friends, and have more exciting memories. I didn't expect to develop life skills or have more self-confidence. But these were benefits from my moving, too. If I had stayed in Florida, or not moved multiple times, these gains would not have been mine.

Are there specific rewards you are expecting when you move? Remember, there will be *unexpected* gains as well. Let's take a look at some of these.

TWELVE MAJOR REWARDS

In the following paragraphs, I will describe some of the benefits gained from moving. Since my personal stories are interwoven into the telling, I will not include a separate section for *How I Did It*.

Reward 1: Knowing What Really Matters

A major change, like moving to a new town, usually results in getting clear about what is important. Moving makes demands on your time, money, and energy and forces choices for these resources. When deciding between one job and another, or between one living arrangement and another, you become aware of what is important to you in these areas. From this awareness, your interests, your future goals, your standard of living, and your relationships are prioritized. This is the clarity needed to live your life with intention and focus.

> *There is peace in being older.*
> *It comes from trying 100 things*
> *And throwing out 98,*
> *Then trying 100 more*
> *Until you've distilled your life down*
> *To pure pleasure.*

CHOOSE TO MOVE

My early moves were done without this clarity of values and interests. They were unfocused and, as a result, less enjoyable. I had new choices but no awareness of what was important to me. I had nothing to guide me in making choices. When I distilled what was really important and enjoyable, then I made smarter choices for the use of my time, money, and energy.

Here's an example from Austin, my first move. Being a newcomer, I accepted invitations to go to live country music performances but didn't really enjoy them. I stepped back and made a list of favorite activities I had enjoyed in the past. Listening to live country music was not on the list. Bird watching was. From that realization, I contacted the Audubon Society and went birding instead. In this way, I made a wiser choice from the new options available in Austin.

As I moved, I also developed strength of purpose. It came from knowing what was important to me. For example, I asked myself why I was willing to live with few possessions or had little commitment to a community. The answer always centered on what I valued at that time. Often it was the freedom and ease of moving to a new town over having a lot of furnishings. Or, I valued the new landscapes over being deeply rooted in the same community. Knowing what I valued the most led to choices that made living more fulfilling and made moving more successful. This self-knowledge was a valuable reward of moving.

Do you remember the *Life's Essentials* list you made? That's your list of what is most important to you. In the course of moving, you can use that list as a guide to see whether changing places has benefited your life. You can also revise the list if moving reveals other aspects of life that have become priorities.

172

Reward 2: Growing Life Skills

Because moving is about surviving and thriving in an unfamiliar landscape, it is an opportunity to develop more life skills. Moving gives you opportunities to make decisions and experience the results. This process produces a set of skills that will stay with you in later endeavors. For example, it will be necessary to keep yourself safe. What actions will you take? You will also need to find a qualified doctor and a skilled mechanic. How will you find them? You will have to stay healthy. Will you exercise and watch your diet? These are life skills. Finding positive, supportive friends is a life skill, too. All these skills plus others will be used and strengthened when you move. If you didn't know how to do these things before you moved, you will certainly learn how after you move! And once mastered, these skills will always be yours, to create the life you want over and over again.

When I moved, I had to create a prosperous life for myself in my new home. I had to develop the skill to safeguard my health, the skill to be happy on my own, and the skill to distinguish between emotionally healthy people and emotionally unhealthy people. I also learned to drive in unfamiliar traffic, to find the nearest health food store, and to wear layers in the winter to keep warm. These are *all* valuable life skills!

Acquiring life skills is an important benefit of moving. The reward is that you become more capable of living the life you want to live and with an increased sense of self-sufficiency.

Reward 3: Gaining Self-Confidence

Moving usually stirs up a beehive of worries. There can be the worry of poverty. A little voice in your head may say, *I will be a bag person if I leave this job.* There can also be the

CHOOSE TO MOVE

worry of rejection, when the voice says, *They won't like me if I don't settle down and have a permanent address*, or the fear of inadequacy, *I can't do it*. These are strong worries and moving will catapult them to center stage where you will have to deal with them.

One day at a time is a simple and effective motto for dealing. Small successes begin to occur and you congratulate yourself with each one. Perhaps the team at work invites you to lunch. *Wow*, you think. *Maybe this new life is going to work! Maybe I won't get fired*. Or you balance your checkbook and find you're in the green! You will begin to believe the move is manageable. You will also begin to believe in your ability to succeed in this new setting. As successes increase, so will your self-confidence. You will be able to laugh at your insecurities. Well, at least you will be able to go to sleep without worrying. If you succeed long enough, you will know in your heart that you certainly can do whatever is required for this move to be a victory.

I had worries to overcome every time I changed places. I worried about having enough money in each new home. Could I find lucrative work? Could I deal with an increased cost of living? I also worried about being alone and not having friends. This worry dominated my first days of a new move because this was a time when I didn't know many people. Then little successes began to happen. I joined interest groups like Audubon and Sierra Club and found like-minded people. I visited farms and found the tastiest blueberries to pick. I also learned that the golden tassels on the top of a corn stalk are not the parts we eat—and I learned to pick the corn ears! My self-confidence increased with these accomplishments. So did the fun!

174

One of my biggest fears was that I wouldn't be able to move myself from place to place. When I learned to drive a U-Haul truck, all those feelings changed. I can tell you, nothing is faster at raising self-confidence than getting behind the wheel of a large, powerful vehicle loaded with all your earthly possessions. There I was, a powerful, self-confident house-carrying turtle!

Through the experience of moving, you *will* gain self-confidence. Increased self-confidence directly reduces worries. And, life is a whole lot easier if you can live it without worrying!

Reward 4: Improved Health

Improved health can also be a reward of moving. If you make an effort to maintain good health with exercise, nutritious food, and rest, you will be rewarded. If you stay active by exploring your new hometown on foot rather than by car, your health will benefit as well. In a new place, maintaining your health may actually be fun. New recreational facilities or the availability of new sports will give you options for activities. In Denver, scenic hiking trails wind through the mountains. In Austin, miles and miles of bike trails exist within the city limits. I enjoyed them all.

A change in weather conditions may also mean more days for outside exercise. Snow for skiing or warm ocean waters for diving will enhance your health if you take advantage of them. A new place may provide these opportunities.

Moving also promotes better health because it motivates you to be a healthier person for your new adventure. You may want to look more attractive or be more active. You will be motivated to show up at your best!

CHOOSE TO MOVE

Reward 5: Gaining a New Awareness of Society and Culture

If leisure travel is considered as educational as a college course, then moving to a new place should be considered a full bachelor's degree! Moving puts you into a whole new world. You will be exposed to new social norms, political views, and local issues. In addition, each place has its own history, commerce, and traditions. Where is trade conducted? Visiting the loading docks in Anchorage showed me steel cranes lifting heavy containers onto ocean going ships and told me a lot about Anchorage commerce. Visiting the warehouses in San Antonio where vegetables are stored and shipped showed me how produce moves through the United States.

Each place will also have its own unique political and ethnical perspectives. The reasons why people vote in Florida are very different from the reasons they vote in Alaska. And what they vote for is very different too. In Florida, you might vote to lower the amount of property tax; in Alaska, you might vote to legalize marijuana. In Portland, you can get signatures on a petition and have *anything* you want voted on. Well, almost. Some areas will be Republican, some will be primarily Democratic. After living in a variety of places, with political, economical, and philosophical differences, you will begin to appreciate just how varied the quilt of our country is.

The differing social perspectives were some of the first things I noticed when I began to move. How did social differences reflect our country's history and how did social inequalities weave together to form one nation? I went to graduate school in Denver to understand the American culture I was experiencing in the cities where I lived. This educational experience changed my social awareness.

176

The Incredible Rewards of Moving

Living with other cultures also increased my social understandings. In Anchorage, a mix of Native Alaskan cultures is seen in the people on the streets. Inupiat and Inuit people, successors of earlier Eskimo people, sell crafts, have homes, hunt moose, and stage festivals in this Far North land. What is the history of these peoples? Where did they come from? Living in Anchorage made me wonder. In San Antonio, lively Mexican music, zesty food, and colorful festivals were plentiful. I interacted with Hispanic people in stores, restaurants, and as neighbors. I wondered what dreams they had for the future.

What was Anchorage like fifty years ago, before it became accessible by highways and fast airlines? Long-time teachers and gold miners in Anchorage told me the stories. What is it like to grow older and to retire in America? My neighbors in a retirement community in San Antonio shared some of their answers. I learned what young men and women expected from a career when I worked with them in Denver. I could not have gotten this social awareness from reading a book or watching a documentary or even from taking seminary courses. I had to live in the place in order to understand these unique perspectives.

Moving compels you to experience other societies and cultures. Through this opportunity, you may begin to see the world around you in a fresh way and re-evaluate your new role in it.

Reward 6: Increasing Financial Prosperity

The Universe smiles on movers. Prosperity on all fronts appears to increase as you move. Moving offers the opportunity to increase your wealth, and your lifestyle options. Through

CHOOSE TO MOVE

moving you learn to make smarter choices, and these smarter choices will lead to increased prosperity on all fronts. This may come gradually, but it has been my experience that it does come.

Moving can introduce you to new opportunities to make money. You can take advantage of new jobs in your new location. And if you are willing to relocate several times, you may have many favorable job choices. Working from home for a company in another town is also widely available. This is called telecommuting. Suppose, though, that you have chosen to move to a town that has fewer jobs which are appropriate for you. This might be an opportunity to expand your creative talents and change your career.

Some of my own moves were the result of lucrative career opportunities. I was able to take advantage of higher salaries in Portland and in Denver. I was also willing to make career changes to new fields.

Increased wealth can come not only from an increased salary, but also from lifestyle choices. You can choose to have a simpler way of life in order to travel or to move again. You can actually make a move financially successful by these choices. For example, when I moved to Anchorage I furnished my apartment from garage sales and slept on an air mattress. The adventure and scenery were so exciting; I didn't care how I lived. In San Diego, I lived with a friend. I saved on the rent, and I also had a companion for sightseeing. In Denver, I existed without my vehicle when it was destroyed in an accident. Because of that decision, I learned to feel comfortable riding buses. In Denver, I lived in a school dormitory for half the rent of urban housing. Because I had the most mag-

178

nificent view of the Rocky Mountains, the size and condition of the apartment were not important. Sometimes I stored my belongings to save the expense of shipping and to be able to rent a smaller living space. Were these choices limiting? Not for me, because they allowed me to be more prosperous.

Reward 7: Opportunities for New Experiences

Moving provides many opportunities for enjoying new experiences. In every town there are ways to try new sports, learn new skills, make new crafts, and explore new locations. It just takes a little courage to go beyond your comfort level and try a new activity. When you do, you may discover a new hobby or a breathtaking view. A country farm may surprise you with the plumpest strawberries. When you find these treasures, you may have found lifelong favorites to enjoy again and again. Truth is, they are everywhere. But in your familiar home environment where you are settled into routines and your circle of friends, you may not search out these new experiences.

Throughout this book, I have shared many of the new interests, hobbies, and locations I have enjoyed when I moved—wildflower photography, ocean snorkeling, fish-fly collecting, local art collecting, line dancing, and organic gardening. I also took out-of-the-ordinary road trips to mountains, gorges, and farmlands. It took courage for me to try new activities and travel unfamiliar roads and these discoveries have been major rewards of my own moving! You can expect to have them, too.

Reward 8: Gaining New Friends and Family

In your new town, there will be opportunities to make new friends and enjoy stimulating activities with them. You will

CHOOSE TO MOVE

meet people who have the same interests as you do, as well as people who have interests you have never considered. Some of these people may become friends. You may create adventures with them, learn from them, and share daily routines.

Along the way, you may also develop deeper bonds with some of the new people you meet. These relationships will become part of your extended family—people with whom you share your life and whom you can trust for support. They may not take the place of your blood relatives, but they will occupy a special place in your life and will see you through the difficult times. These relationships can survive even if distance separates the two of you later. This is a wonderful reward of moving.

I always moved for the scenery of a place. But what I got in addition were incredible people who became my friends, hosts, and colleagues. Today many of these people are still in my life even though I have moved away from the towns where we first met.

Reward 9: Anonymity

Not many people know you when you first arrive in town. Therefore, moving can be an opportunity to re-create yourself. You can change the way you dress, style your hair differently, get a body piercing, or change your political views—you can change almost everything about appearance! The changes are all in good fun and all a way to explore more of your potential. Anonymity can provide a safe space for these changes.

You can be a beginner at a new sport or craft and enjoy learning at your own pace. You could try your hand at golf or rock climbing while you are a newcomer and do it just for

180

fun. No one who knows you will be watching. What fun to try without inhibition!

Being new in town gave me freedom to try some things I had always wanted to do. Some of them were very daring. In several towns, I tried new sports because I didn't have to worry about who would see me. I also took the opportunity to color my hair and take ballet lessons. I liked the new me these changes produced.

Anonymity can be rewarding if you use it for exploring your fantasies.

Reward 10: Being Your Own Authority

Moving puts you in the driver's seat of your life. It is a time when you have to make many decisions and rely on your own judgment. If you haven't done much of this before, then moving will give you the chance to practice these skills and will reward you with wiser judgment and stronger life-skills.

Consider the challenge of what to take with you if you move. Each person planning a move has to face this challenge. As we discovered in Chapter 2, these aren't straightforward decisions. But when you are finished deciding which treasures to take and which to leave behind, you will feel a sense of accomplishment. And this feeling will spill over to other areas. You may find yourself making wiser decisions about housing, jobs, and friends. Moving will give you the authority to make decisions that prosper your life.

Reward 11: Expanding Your Dreams

The moving process can lift your sights beyond the tedium of the current moment to see tomorrow with its potential for success. This longer view may come because you are open to new possibilities. It is no longer a far stretch to see the future and your dreams coming true. You can see yourself taking the African safari or writing a best-selling novel. You can imagine becoming a top executive at your company or even starting your own business. These visions are a reward of moving. Once you are uprooted, there is no limit to the dreams you can imagine and attain! This reward can also get you into serious trouble. New dreams can also lead to more exploring!

When I made the first move, I expected it to be the *first* and *last*. As I began to enjoy changing places, I entertained visions of more moves to other appealing places. Each move was first conceived as a dream, and then the dream was put into action. If I had stayed in Florida, I would not have entertained those dreams. Expanding dreams is an amazing reward of moving.

Reward 12: Contentment

Somewhere in the moving process a sense of contentment begins to surface. I'm not sure if it's contentment to be where you are, or contentment to be who you are. I suspect it's the latter. Whichever it is, it is a feeling that all is right with the world, and all is right with you. It is a peaceful feeling that comes after struggles for companionship, amusement, or a sense of belonging. It seems to come from the willingness to do your best and be satisfied with the outcome.

When I was in Denver, I did my best to enjoy the snowy winter. I bought warm clothes, walked in the icy mush, and asked for help when I needed it. Contentment came that winter. These are the notes I wrote in my journal:

The best times in Denver were spent cozied up in socks in my warm, old dormitory apartment during the snowy winter. In the midst of one heavy snowstorm, I peeped periodically out through a slit in the blinds to see the falling snow being reflected in the streetlights. "Let it snow!" I shouted, "I have my books, my writing, myself to enjoy."

Each time I have moved, the feelings of contentment and serenity have gotten stronger. I trust the world more because I trust myself more. I carry my home and my peace with me, like a snail with its shell. Wherever I am *is* my home and the people I meet are my friends. Whatever art, or decorations, or clothes I buy are just icing on the cake of having a sense of home and family wherever in the world I choose to go.

IN SUMMARY

The rewards are many when you move to a new place. For each person, these rewards will be different. Some will be expected, and many will be unexpected and far richer than you could have envisioned. It is these rewards that make all the efforts and difficulties of moving worthwhile.

CHOOSE TO MOVE

OTHER QUESTIONS TO THINK ABOUT

1. *Are the rewards I discussed the ones you expected to get from making a move? If not, what rewards do you expect to get?*

2. *Do any of these rewards make you smile? Do any of them resonate with you enough to say, "I would move for that reward"?*

3. *What benefits would you expect from moving that weren't discussed here?*

4. *Sometimes you don't recognize rewards like these until you've had them awhile. How would you know if you had more self-confidence or were more your own authority?*

5. *Moving doesn't have to be the only change you make. What new dreams would you entertain if you moved? New career? New car? Marriage? Entertain your wildest fantasy.*

6. *What new activity would you try or what personal change would you make if you had no one to discourage you?*

7. *How would you know if you were content? What in your life would matter more and what in your life would matter less?*

184

9

Thriving Anywhere

CONSIDER THIS ...

Now that we have discussed the decision to move, the hardships moving involves, and the beneficial rewards moving offers, one more topic needs addressing. Do I stay put or move again?

You can choose to stay where you are, either for a long time or a short time. Or, you can choose to pack up everything and go back to the place you left—for a short time, or a long time. Or you can move again to a new location. The information in this chapter will help you be better equipped to make these decisions about moving or staying.

Staying Where You Are

Not so long ago, a move to a new location was usually a permanent change. Moving was difficult and not undertaken lightly. It was done because the job was transferred, because other family members moved, or because of health concerns. Today, however, moving can be by choice and it need not be permanent. So, the reasons to stay will be different than they used to be.

The main incentive to stay is to enjoy the successes you have created in your new hometown. Perhaps you have found like-minded friends and feel you belong at last. Perhaps you have learned to enjoy winter sports and this town offers top-quality winter recreation. Perhaps you have a well-paying job and are able to have more money. Staying could be a wise decision in these circumstances.

> *Reflections of a Move*
>
> *In my apartment*
> *In my new town*
> *I hung all my art*
> *Laid down bright rugs*
> *And waited.*
> *No one came.*
> *So I read and toured*
> *And joined clubs*
> *And made a life.*
>
> *Now I'm leaving.*
> *My art is neatly boxed*
> *The refrigerator is empty*
> *And my rugs are rolled.*
> *My apartment is bare*
> *But I'm having a party.*
> *All my friends are here*
> *To celebrate, to wish me well*
> *And to say good-bye.*
> *– Portland*

How long will you stay? Perhaps you will decide to stay permanently. In this case you might want to buy your own home or enroll in school for an additional degree. On the other hand, you might decide to stay for only six months and then re-evaluate your decision.

In my own moving experiences, I would *try on* the staying option. After a year in a new town, I would commit to staying for four or six more months. If I were still content at the end of the period, then I would put away the moving boxes. If not, it was time for me to move again. I needed to take this decision in small pieces because it was an overwhelming choice to make.

MOVING BACK TO YOUR HOMETOWN

Moving back is usually easier than moving to a new place because you know what awaits you at the other end. The transition to familiar neighborhoods and climate will be much quicker. Friends and activities will help you reconnect. However, I want to remind you that some aspects of your life back home will be different from what they were before. Perhaps you are returning with improved finances and you can afford to live in a nicer neighborhood. Or perhaps you are returning married when you left single. Some changes will make the old hometown a more enjoyable place than it was before.

Other changes will take away what prospered you here. For example, your best friend moved away while you were gone. Perhaps the traffic congestion has worsened. Whatever the change, things will be different when you return. Some adjustment to these changes will be necessary.

If you haven't enjoyed being in the new town you chose, moving back to what's familiar may be a more satisfying choice. Perhaps the weather was too hot or too cold, or perhaps the well-paying job you went for ended after a few months. Or maybe you have come to appreciate the value of life in the old hometown. While living in Austin, I began to realize the value of my friends and lifestyle in Orlando so I moved back to the town I left in Florida. I reconnected with my supportive friends and resumed church and social activities. I even took up residence in the same house since I had rented it while I was away. Going back will always be an option for you.

CHOOSE TO MOVE

In some cases, moving back may have compelling incentives. Perhaps a family member becomes gravely ill, or your old company offers you twice your former salary to return. Perhaps you inherit land ideal for building your dream house. Although you do have a choice, these circumstances may produce a strong tug to return.

MOVING TO A NEW PLACE

Obviously, I am biased in the direction of moving again since I moved many times. My moves were more than I had ever planned and enriching adventures each time. But what about you? Could you, would you ever decide to move again? Could you go through the agonizing loneliness and sheer hard labor of relocating to another unfamiliar place? The choice to move again is equally as valid as the decision to stay or to move back.

The goal to move again may be to experience another part of the world. Moving just for the fun of it is definitely okay, especially now that you have the confidence and moving experience to take with you. Did you save your copy of *Places Rated Almanac*? You may need it again if you decide to live in another distinctive city or town.

One incentive to move again may be to take advantage of prospering opportunities. Perhaps a lucrative job has been offered or you want to live near someone special. In these cases, the decision to move may be easy to make, and the move itself may be easier, because you have moved once before and you know what to expect.

The good news is that the second move is easier than the first one. The same resources will be needed, the same personal strengths will be required that were needed for your first move. But there's a difference between choosing to move for the first time and choosing to move again. That difference is you. You are now more experienced and you have more self-confidence. You will get out and explore earlier, you will make friends easier, and you will be more open to the unique features of your new hometown that make it special. All these positive changes will make this subsequent move easier than the first one.

Choosing to move again may be difficult. Experiencing success and prosperity through moving can foster inertia. You may want to stay where you are because life is good. Will you want to give it all up to move again? Considering a second move may also be difficult because you know what hard work moving requires. You know the loneliness and frustrations it involves. Hopefully, you feel your move has been worthwhile despite these and you might even consider doing it again! As you can see, this second-time-around decision-making process can get very thorny, depending on your successes, your attitude, and your opportunities.

OTHER INFLUENCING FACTORS

The decision to stay or to move again will be influenced by many factors. Money, health, and putting down roots have to be considered when thinking of moving again. What motivates you to do it again? What payoffs and losses do you anticipate? Here are more questions to consider as you think of staying, or moving.

Money

How healthy is your financial situation? Do you have more money as a result of the previous move or has your money supply dwindled? If it has dwindled and you have less money or more expenses than before the move, determine if that is a temporary situation, caused by moving expenses or a house purchase, or if you are falling short in your new venture. Don't let money be the deciding issue in a decision to move, but do seriously consider it. Both your present financial circumstances and your potential for income in a new town must be measured. The bottom line for money and moving is: Have enough money to enjoy the experience of moving.

Emotional and Physical Health

How have your state of mind, your physical health, and your emotions fared since you moved to a new place? These will all be affected by a move. Moving takes a lot of energy. It is hard work to manage, move, and arrange yourself in a new town. Do you have the energy to move again?

Leaving and separations can take a toll on emotional health. How many times can you bid farewell and remain sane? This is very important to monitor. Even though I enjoyed the new experiences of moving, leaving the people and places I enjoyed was always sad. To offset this, I maintained a continuity of friendships and familiar activities that would promote a positive outlook in a new place.

It is possible to lessen the losses from moving. You can relocate to places where friends or family already live. In that way, some connections are already in place. Or you can get a friend to move with you. *My* friends certainly have been asked many times! So far no one has agreed. What resources do you have for lessening your losses if you decide to move again?

Growing Roots

Moving raises the question of having a long-term involvement in a community. Moving and long-term *anything* are mutually exclusive goals. You won't have a long-term connection to a community if you have only resided there for a few years. Whether you want to continue to move depends on your answers to these questions—Is it time to put down roots? Do you need to nest or do you need to fly?

At every juncture in this process, take your pulse on this issue. And when your pulse tells you to stay and grow in one community, then your moving days are over.

Personal Goals

What personal goals would be achieved if you moved again? Which ones would be realized by staying? If your goal is to experience a variety of cities and towns by living in them, then moving is the only way to meet this goal. If you want to build a house and live by the ocean, then moving to the coast may be the best choice. Perhaps all your personal goals were met by the first move and nothing significant would be gained by moving again. On the other hand, new ambitions can be flamed by a successful move, and one of these ambitions could be to live in other extraordinary locations. Reviewing the list of rewards for moving discussed in Chapter 8 may be helpful. These potential rewards can be goals for future moves.

One of my goals for moving was to be able to live in any new place and come to feel it was my home. I needed to move more than once to achieve this. Another goal was to

191

CHOOSE TO MOVE

experience other cultures and societies. One move wasn't enough to satisfy this goal either. Successive moves were necessary to achieve these goals.

Motivation and Desire

I am always amused when someone says to me, "I would move, too, if it weren't for my children being in school/my wife's (husband's) job/owning a house/my job/the dog/the weather/the old car." I don't believe a word of it. If you truly want to move, you will find a way. And if you want to stay, you will find a way for that, too.

I keep a message on my refrigerator that reads "Desires of the heart are good for they are the urging of The Universe to move us forward to our higher self." These desires of the heart push us to action. Sometimes this action is to relocate to another town. Sometimes these desires make us quite content to stay put.

Do you dream about living in a new place? How passionate do you feel about making a change? How restless are you? See if this quote from *The Simple Living Guide* resonates with you: "Sometimes my yearning for open skies has gotten so bad that I get a lump in my throat and a tear in my eye when I see an airplane flying overhead. I'm very sorry I'm not in it, going somewhere." Your desires and dreams influence your decision to stay or move again.

What Others Think

I was once asked why I couldn't put down roots. It was very hurtful at the moment, because I wanted my lifestyle to be accepted in my new community. But I came to realize not everyone would applaud me for moving and not settling down.

THRIVING ANYWHERE

I have learned to dismiss what others think about how I live my life. They have their own agendas and growth schedules. I have mine. And you will have yours. Nothing anyone thinks or says about your decisions matters. Not even what is written in this book. Remember that.

THE WORLD IS AS WE ARE

Have you heard the story of the two newcomers? I told this story in Chapter 1. It bears repeating, now that you are making the decision to move again. So, there are two newcomers. Each was asked where they came from and how they liked it. The first newcomer replied, "I came from Chickaloon City and I hated it. The weather is too cold, the people unfriendly, and moose ate my vegetable garden."

The second newcomer was asked the same questions. Their reply was, "I came from Chickaloon City and it's a fantastic town. We can ski in the winter, people help each other shoveling snow, and the moose hunting is superb."

The point is: Where you are is what you bring with you. If you didn't like your last new place, you are more likely to dislike this one. And if you liked the last one, you will probably like the new one just fine. When we move, we bring with us *all* our baggage, the packed stuff as well as the stuff in our heads.

I learned this slowly as I moved from place to place. I found out home was where I was, not better or worse than before. And I learned being happy was an inside job and not about my address. If I needed disappointments, I found people and circumstances everywhere to fulfill that need. And if I needed to experience joy, I found that too. Unfulfilled needs, disappointments, and loneliness are in every town just as are

193

happy surprises, exciting outings, and incredible friends. What you find in any particular setting is what you go looking for. Remember this when you are deciding to stay, move back, or move on.

HOW I DID IT

Have you been wondering, as you read this book, *Why in the world did she move so much?* I am about to answer that question. I hope after you read about the attitudes I had and the circumstances that I experienced, you will agree that moving was a prospering choice for me.

In the Beginning

In the beginning, I considered moving very cautiously. Up to the time I turned fifty, I had lived my entire life in Florida. Certainly I had traveled, but I had never moved more than one hundred miles from my hometown and never alone. Therefore, the first decision to move a cat, some belongings, and myself was a daunting one. I did not intend to do it again and again! However, once I moved, I began to grow the skills I needed to be successful and I enjoyed the adventure of living in a new town. So, I kept moving.

I consider the number of moves I have made to be unusual. I'm certainly not advocating that everyone move this much. I continued to move because the opportunity to experience a new place with all its foods, art, activities, and politics was immensely more alluring to me than staying in one place. Relocating was easy when I reduced my household belongings and learned to pack efficiently. It was also financially possible because I chose large cities where I could find work in my field.

My series of moves was not the result of a master plan made in Orlando, or even in Austin. Rather it was the result of a succession of life events. Each move was inspired and undertaken for reasons that were right at the time. Each move was rewarding and exciting and expansive.

My motives for the first move to Austin are explained in detail in the first chapter. In the sections that follow, I will share my reasons for other moves to Gainesville, Anchorage, San Diego, Portland, Denver, San Antonio, back to Austin, and beyond.

SECOND MOVE-ORLANDO TO GAINESVILLE

I moved to Gainesville because the first move to Austin had been harder than I expected. It was traumatic for me to live in an unfamiliar place. I just didn't have the skills needed at that point, so I moved back to my hometown. I knew that I still didn't want to live in Orlando and I also knew I didn't have my moving legs yet. I studied *Places Rated Almanac* and chose Gainesville for my next move. It was close enough to my home in Orlando that I could return on weekends. This was a more practical move for someone like me who was inexperienced in making a home and finding new friends.

Eventually, I wanted to explore beyond Florida and try long-distance moving again.

THIRD MOVE-ORLANDO TO ANCHORAGE

I moved to Anchorage for the adventure. It was a place I loved visiting and one I wanted to experience as a local resident. This was the first time I chose to move based on the place itself, not because it was close or convenient.

Anchorage is an incredibly unique town in Alaska. One half is surrounded by mountains, some spewing ash and smoke. Ocean inlets with whales, seals, and salmon surround the other half. In the spring, these salmon make their last journey into fresh water streams and rivers, spawn, and die. Moose roam the streets. All seasons but winter are short. Living is in the moment and newcomers are welcomed.

To make the move, I left all my belongings behind, either stored or sold. It was too exciting an adventure to pass up and my adult son decided to join me. With his support, I was very happy. We arrived in Anchorage in early spring, just after the roads were free of snow. My commitment was to stay as long as I could endure the weather.

By the time November arrived in Anchorage, several inches of snow were on the ground, and the days were noticeably shorter. Ice coated the roads and sidewalks. *How long could I take this*? I kept wondering. Each week I would say to Eric, "Maybe I'll go this week," but I hoped I could adjust. Just before Thanksgiving, my company offered to transfer me to San Diego and I accepted.

Fourth Move-Anchorage to San Diego

I moved to San Diego because I had to. I was not a winter survivor. I had a friend who offered me a place to stay. I looked forward to sunny and bright San Diego weather. On the downside, there would be no moose!

After a few weeks in San Diego, it appeared that everyone who loved sunshine had moved there. And they all brought their cars! After being in Anchorage, I was stunned by so many people and so much traffic. Thanksgiving came and went. It never rained a drop. Then Christmas arrived and with it, an offer that doubled my current salary.

FIFTH MOVE-SAN DIEGO TO PORTLAND

I moved to Hillsboro, a suburb of Portland, for the opportunity to work for Intel and earn a lot of money. In addition, Oregon had been on my list of places to visit and moving met this goal. This was the first move I had done on my own. I did not have friends or family waiting. And most amazing of all, I had never stepped foot in the state of Oregon! I didn't know what to expect.

What a wonderful surprise I got! The landscape was gorgeous. Fields of red clover, sixty-foot Douglas fir trees, and patterned rolling hills were to become my new home. In the distance were snow-capped mountains. Succulent, fresh fruits and vegetables ripened each month. I was so pleased with my choice. I didn't stop loving this countryside even when a monumental flood came one spring, covering the streets of Portland and toppling the trees.

I lived in Hillsboro for twenty-one months. The friendships I made were unique and lasting. I have vivid memories: of staying in the home of a couple when I lost electricity in my apartment; of being fetched after a late class by a colleague from India when my taxi did not arrive; of vegetable gardening with Irene; of being challenged by games of rummy tiles with birding friends; and of a farewell visit to my favorite farmers' market with three fantastic, attractive female friends. On all accounts, this was a move with many successes—so many that the idea of writing a book about them formed in my mind!

Those successes motivated me to dream again about fulfilling other, wilder dreams like attending seminary.

Sixth Move-Portland to Denver

I moved to Denver to attend seminary and study religion. After twenty-one months on the frontlines of Intel and almost thirty years of working in the high-tech field, I was ready for a change. I had saved enough money for my school expenses so I applied and was accepted to Iliff School of Theology. At fifty-five, I was a freshman seminary student studying about social injustices!

I began to understand our society in new ways. I finished my first year with all A's and pride in my accomplishments. Writing on this book slowed.

When I took a job downtown, my friends were a strange mix. Some were from seminary, liberals who wanted to change the system, and some from my workplace, conservative sports enthusiasts who were content with the status quo.

Denver never felt like my kind of place, even though I remained for over a year and a half. Maybe it was the mountains I didn't particularly enjoy. Maybe it was the skiing I never learned. Or maybe it was just having winter at all, complete with snow and ice. Whatever it was, I began to open *Places Rated Almanac* again for relocation ideas. Only Honolulu remained as a dream town. However, it seemed too far and too foreign to do alone. The feeling of wanting to settle down still nagged at me, too.

When I expressed a desire to live elsewhere, my company offered to let me telecommute from anywhere I chose to live. That was the impetus I needed to pack my belongings into a U-Haul and head for Texas. But on the way, I spent three summer months back in my beloved Portland, picking strawberries and apples, reconnecting with friends and telecommuting to Denver.

Seventh Move-Denver to San Antonio

I moved to San Antonio for its weather, diverse population, and proximity to Austin and my brother. I hoped *this* would be my permanent home. Once again I expected to have winters without snow. I expected to see my brother, but not on a daily basis. What I didn't expect were all the festivals and Mariachi music from the Hispanic population in San Antonio. These were spicy surprises!

Getting to Texas was easy with the U-Haul and a friend for copilot. I had a furnished house to rent in a quiet, retirement neighborhood. The day after I arrived, the worst flood in twenty years rolled over south-central Texas and overflowed the rivers into the streets of San Antonio and Austin. It forced me to get to know my neighbors in a hurry!

I continued to make monthly trips back to the office in Denver. Since I worked at home in San Antonio, I quickly made friends with my retired neighbors who were also home during the day. I found players for rummy tiles again. Life was good. Moving again seemed improbable. Then my brother began to urge me to return to Austin. Not only would I be nearer to him but I also could find a job in my field and stop telecommuting. Did I have one more move in me?

EIGHTH MOVE-SAN ANTONIO TO AUSTIN

Going back to Austin was a completion of the moving cycle that had started nine years before. Going back to the first place I had moved was very revealing. It showed me how much courage and how many skills I had acquired. This time, moving to Austin was an easy success. I knew my way around town. I met people easily and I found the like-minded friends I had been seeking in San Antonio. I also found a high cost of living and a job that paid for it. Winters were warm and the days were sunny. Friends came to visit my art-filled apartment and the relationship with my brother, Paul, flourished. The move to Austin was as prospering as moving gets.

I unpacked everything I brought from Denver. *Every single thing*. It was the first time I had been able to do that since I left Portland, two years earlier. Most of my boxed possessions were not unpacked in Denver or in San Antonio. There had not been enough space in the college dormitory or in the furnished house. Now, over two years later, I had some humorous surprises. I still had the portable heater from Anchorage I had used on chilly November days. I stepped out of many a warm shower into the glow from that heater! I unpacked the fan I had bought in Portland for the three days of blistering weather that occurs each summer. It had been the last fan for sale at Wal-Mart. I also found the humidifier I bought in Denver to combat the dry air.

In Austin, I didn't need a heater, fan, or humidifier. And yet, it was hard for me to resist repacking them into their custom boxes, ready for the next daring move. They had all been very important to my comfort at one time. In the future, would I want warm air, moving air, or moist air? In the end, only the heater was sent to the charity shelter. The fan and the humidifier travel on.

AUSTIN TO HONOLULU

Honolulu? Where did that come from? Well, guess what—tonight I finalized plans to move to Honolulu. I leave in two months. I am both excited and scared. This is a dream come true. I expect to have *many* visitors and I expect Eric to share a second bedroom for a few months. I plan to visit South Pacific islands that will be nearer here than to the mainland. I also plan this to be my last great move.

I can't sleep because the lists are swirling around in my head. So much will need to be done—forward mail to an unknown address, move furnishings into storage, say good-byes, find a job, dispose of a vehicle—so much to think about. Where do I begin? That's easy—I begin by reading the first chapter of this book!

IN SUMMARY

Staying in one place can be richly rewarding after moving. And moving again can be just as wonderful an experience as it was the first time. You will know, after examining your circumstances, goals, and motives, whether staying, moving back, or moving on is the right decision for you. Be sure the choice is a positive, enhancing experience motivated by a spirit of adventure and a desire to grow. Put your happiness and well being first. Whether you stay or move again, I offer my sincerest best wishes to you for success!

CHOOSE TO MOVE

OTHER QUESTIONS TO THINK ABOUT

1. *Is there a section of the country that is calling to you other than where you now live? Where have you always wanted to live?*

2. *Suppose you had all the money you needed. Where would you live?*

3. *What do you like about where you live now?*

4. *Is making a decision hard for you? Is fear involved when choosing between options?*

5. *Does having a place to call home and living in the same community for a long time appeal to you*

6. *Are there voices in your life, either real or in your head that discourage you from moving? Can you see from my experiences the times when these voices need to be thanked but ignored, times when moving is worth the effort and risks?*

7. *If you could have one more exciting adventure, what would it be? Why are you waiting?*

202

Epilogue

In All the Places

I taught farm workers English;
walked with a suicidal neighbor;
laughed with an abandoned cat;
showed a loner her partnering side;
brought friends to festivals;
ate tomatoes in my garden;
put fishing flies on my visor;
ate curry with colleagues;
walked someone's Arabian baby;
took a friend to climb a glacier;
photographed pigs at the fair;
thanked the postal workers in letters to the editor;
gave a mother permission to leave work for her children;
brought laughter during gray days;
played rummy tiles with octogenarians;
gave blessings to whales.

I gave blessings all around.
Now, like the sun,
I'm moving on.

Bibliography

Carlisle, Ellen, *Smooth Moves*, Teacup Press, Charlotte, NC, 1999. Simple tips from the author who has moved eight times to seven states.

Fritz, Robert, *Creating*, Fawcett Columbine, New York, NY, 1991. Shows how to master the creative process in order to open new possibilities.

Goodwin, Cathy, *Making the Big Move: How to Transform Relocation into a Creative Life Transition*, New Harbinger Publishers, Oakland, CA, 1999. A useful resource for coping with the transitions of moving.

Howells, John, *Where to Retire*, The Globe Pequot Press, Guildford, CT, 2003. Designed for those approaching retirement, this book focuses on where to retire.

Luhrs, Janet, *The Simple Living Guide*, Broadway Books, New York, NY, 1997. A sourcebook for less stressful, more joyful living.

Otterbourg, Robert K, *Retire & Thrive*, Kiplinger Books, Wash. D.C., 2003. Remarkable people, age 50+, share creative, profitable retirement strategies.

Ramsey, Dan, *The Complete Idiot's Guide to Smart Moving*, Alpha Books, New York, NY, 1998. Covers all areas of the moving process in easy to follow chapters.

Roman, Beverly and John Howells, *Insider's Guide to Relocation*, Globe Pequot Press, Guilford, CT, 2004. Helpful information for domestic as well as international relocation.

Savageau, David, *Places Rated Almanac*, Hungry Minds, New York, NY, 2000. A guide to 354 metropolitan areas in the United States and Canada ranked by cost of living, crime, climate, and recreational activities. Tremendously useful resource!

Savageau, David, *Retirement Places Rated*, Macmillan, New York, NY, 1999. Rates 180 retirement areas by living costs, climate, services, crime, work opportunities and recreation.

Sperling, Bert and Peter Sander, *Cities Ranked and Rated*, Wiley Publishing, Inc., New York, NY, 2004. This new resource ranks over 400 cities by several important factors.

Zelinski, Ernie J., *The Joy of Not Working*, Ten Speed Press, Toronto, Canada, 2003. Speaks to retired, unemployed, or overworked people seeking change.